How to Coach
Basketball

Jerry Phipps

How to Coach Basketball
Copyright © 2021 G.H. Phipps
ISBN 978-1-970153-30-9
Library of Congress: 2021911732

All rights reserved. No part of this book may be reproduced, stored in a retrieval system, or transmitted in any form or by any means without the prior written permission of the author, except by a reviewer who may quote brief passages in a review printed in a newspaper, magazine, or journal.

La Maison Publishing, Inc.

Maison

Vero Beach, Florida
The Hibiscus City
lamaisonpublishing@gmail.com

DEDICATION

*I dedicate this book to my wife, Joanie,
for her diligence and patience in
aiding me to complete this work.*

*Additionally, I include all my former
players, whose performances were the hallmark
of our teams' successes.*

INTRODUCTION

Why write a book on coaching basketball? To attempt to partially answer this question, let me begin by stating, I was a head high school and junior college basketball coach for 36 years. During this time, I achieved a winning percentage of close to 80 percent. I also served as a volunteer and assistant coach for 10 seasons. Since retirement, I have had the desire to write a book on coaching the sport I spent a career "X-ing" and "O-ing." My hope is to make some contribution to a game that I have grown to love and respect over the years.

Toni Morrison, Nobel Prize winning author, was quoted, "If there is a book that you want to read, and it hasn't been written yet, then you must write it." With this quote in mind, I decided to direct my literary attention toward the novice coach. This work is certainly not an attempt to say, "This is the only and best way to coach basketball." There are many theories and methods of teaching the game that exist. No single person possesses them entirely and no single book is all-inclusive. Therefore, if some concepts and ideas are omitted from these pages, do not conclude I have rejected them. I merely hope that some of my thoughts and methods, based on many years of experience, can be beneficial to others starting to coach this wonderful game. Maybe even the veteran, "seen-it-all" coach, can pick up a trick or two. As you read this book, pick out what you like, and ignore what you do not. Just remember, basketball is a great game that has stood the test of time since Dr. Naismith. Be true to it!

These days there are countless "how to" books on the market. As I attempted to label this endeavor, I pondered several potential titles. Then, one night as I lay awake in bed, it occurred to me, "Keep it simple, stupid!" Since there are many books telling us how to fix our cars, cook our meals, beautify our lawns, build a deck and limitless others, why not one simply saying, "How to Coach Basketball"? So, I did!

Contents

CHAPTER 1 1
   ADOPT A COACHING PHILOSOPHY 1
CHAPTER 2 5
   THE INFLUENCE OF THE COACH............................ 5
CHAPTER 3 10
   SOME QUALIFICATIONS OF A COACH 10
CHAPTER 4 17
   TERMINOLOGY 17
CHAPTER 5 26
   MY COACHING PHILOSOPHY 26
CHAPTER 6 34
   DEFENSE #1, OFFENSE #2... 34
CHAPTER 7 39
   INDIVIDUAL MAN-TO-MAN DEFENSIVE
   FOOTWORK FUNDAMENTALS 39
CHAPTER 8 51
   TEAM MAN-TO-MAN DEFENSIVE
   FUNDAMENTALS 51
CHAPTER 9 62
   MAN-TO-MAN POST DEFENSE............................... 62
CHAPTER 10 67
   EARLY SEASON PRACTICE DRILLLS 67

CHAPTER 11 84
SOME ZONE DEFENSIVE SUGGESTIONS 84
CHAPTER 12 92
GENERAL OFFENSIVE FUNDAMENTALS AND TECHNIQUES 92
CHAPTER 13 99
ATTACKING MAN-TO-MAN DEFENSES 99
CHAPTER 14 110
ATTACKING ZONE DEFENSES 110
CHAPTER 15 118
HOW TO BEAT THE FULL COURT ZONE PRESS DEFENSE 118
CHAPTER 16 135
SWISH… HOW TO PUT A ROUND BALL THROUGH AN ORANGE CIRCLE 135
CHAPTER 17 142
MISCELLANEOUS DRILLS 142
CHAPTER 18 155
DEFENSIVE NUMBERING SYSTEM 155
CHAPTER 19 159
SPECIAL SITUATIONS & DIVERSE MINUTIA ... 159
CHAPTER 20 174
SOME OFF THE COURT NECESSARY ITEMS 174
CHAPTER 21 179
MOTIVATION AND QUOTES 179

CHAPTER 22 - Diagrams 184
    SHELL DRILL 184
    2-1-2 ZONE SLIDES 188
    1-3-1 ZONE SLIDES 192
    T-DEFENSE FROM 2-3 ZONE 196
    T-DEFENSE FROM 1-3-1 ZONE 197
    BLUE OFFENSE 198
    CUT & HOOK BACK 200
    SET UP & MOVES TO BEAT ZONE PRESS 202
EPILOGUE 207
ABOUT THE AUTHOR 215

CHAPTER 1

ADOPT A COACHING PHILOSOPHY

Webster's dictionary defines philosophy as "A theory underlying or regarding a sphere of activity or thought." As applied to coaching basketball, you are better prepared if you possess a definite approach to the game. What you believe to be important offensively and defensively will and should reflect your attitudes toward the sport. Furthermore, it should dictate the kind of coaching methods you use. Analyze yourself and adopt a "theory underlying this sphere of activity," that is, basketball, at least generally, if not specifically in every aspect. Then, be sure to communicate this wisdom to your team. Let them know what you believe and what you will emphasize through instruction. I will relate some of my own philosophy in a later chapter.

In my opinion, for a coach to perform their best, they must be true to oneself. I do not think it is prudent to attempt to imitate others. Dean Smith, a long-time successful coach at the University of North Carolina, was, to me, an excellent coach to learn from in my early days. Did I simulate some of his drills, bits of his offense, and parts of his defensive structure? Of course, I did! His, as well as other respected coaches during my career. However, did I try to be Dean Smith or any other coach? Absolutely not! Dispositions and the totality of a person's experience, knowledge, and education are never identical as we compare individuals. One is phlegmatic, another high-strung, one is mild-mannered, another demanding and hard driving; one may be kind and personal; another somewhat vehement and excitable, one may be encouraging and complimentary, while another prone to expressing severe judgments and criticisms. People are different, so are basketball coaches.

In summary, from study, readings, and observations, try to find valuable and useful strategies that you can incorporate into your philosophy. However, pick and choose carefully, based on whether or not the principles of others fit your own to help a more effective and harmonious "you." Yes, to thy own self be true. Be yourself!

As you adopt your philosophy of coaching, I pause here to offer an observation that I consider an oversight by some coaches, especially the inexperienced ones. There are several steps of expertise on the basketball ladder of competition, i.e., pick-up games, recreation events, club games, high school junior varsity and varsity, junior college and four-year college level, and finally the professional pinnacle. Even the college systems have different segments. They are divisions III, II, and I. Division I sub-dividing further into lower, mid-major, and major.

The game has some consistencies on every level. The basket is 10 feet high. The court is a rectangle of varying widths and lengths. Many of the rules, with some exceptions, are the same or similar. The length of the game may differ, but a timing clock is always involved. A shot clock is used in college and professional circles, but not on the male high school level.

However, with these noted comparable similarities, there are gross differences in how the game is coached and played. Of course, on the upper levels of college and professional arenas, the abilities of the players are exceedingly better as the players are bigger, stronger, faster, taller, and more experienced. My point in mentioning these facts is to inform the untutored and naïve coaches on the lower scale of the basketball spectrum. Do not attempt to emulate and coach patterns of play used on the upper plane of the games. Your players are playing basketball but at a much lower sense of abilities, both mentally and physically, to perform. Therefore, be ever cognizant of those limited abilities and coach, practice, and drill accordingly.

At the lower ranks, I obsessively believe it is not only important but a necessity to emphasize the fundamentals of the game. Not just once in a while when the mood strikes you, but in some form during each and every practice session! What are the fundamentals? The list certainly includes ball-handling, pass-catching, dribbling, shooting lay-ups and jump shots, playing without the ball, defensive footwork and movements, proper screening and use thereof, and blocking out for defensive rebounds. All sports' skills are grounded in the basics. Your team will not be successful without an acceptable degree of talent in these areas. It does not happen magically. Practice! Practice! Practice! More practice is the only means to the reality of skillfulness. How does any musician become a master of his or her instrument? Diligence, patience, work, perseverance, practice, and any other synonyms one can think of.

What seems to occur is for inexperienced coaches to think that offensive play patterns are the antidote for inferior team play. As a result, they add more and more to cure the ailment, which is a mistake. Basic rudiments of basketball are the backbone for any good team. Practice, emphasize and drill them at every session. Master the essentials and coach at the abilities of your players. An overcrowded playbook is not the magic formula for winning basketball. EXECUTION AND SIMPLICITY USUALLY IS!!

CHAPTER 2

THE INFLUENCE OF THE COACH

The coach's tutelage is the primary catalyst, which provokes the benefits that will be transferred to the players through their participation in basketball. The coach is a guardian, a guide, a protector, a disciplinarian, and a teacher. They wield a powerful influence in the trusteeship over the players. To "make the team" or "to get to play," some individuals will submit to almost any demand of the coach. Be sure to use your authority to affect or alter change in the players in the most positive way possible.

Coach-player relationships should be such that a lasting, wholesome influence is created. Since my retirement, I have received numerous emails, phone calls, and letters from former players praising me for my teachings that have guided them as they live out their post-basketball days. Believe me. These are the kinds of rewards that teachers and coaches covet and treasure. A coach may be stern, dignified, and formal, or may be cordial, personal, and informal as befits their own personality. I feel players do not have to "like" the coach. Many will not, based on the demands and discipline of the coach during their playing tenure. However, I steadfastly believe they have to RESPECT the coach.

To earn, and it must be earned, this kind of relationship, a coach, must be a person of high standards. It is better to lead by example than by edict or misuse of authority. To begin, they must demonstrate a thorough knowledge of what is being taught. Be definite and the master of your subject matter. Do not attempt to "fake" what you are not sure of or do not know. This procedure will come back to haunt you and your team. If your knowledge of the game is limited, teach what you have confidence in and keep it simple. Your expertise will improve over time with study and experience.

During my coaching career, I did not believe in establishing a long list of rules for players to obey. Some are necessary and obvious. However, it is extremely important to enforce what rules you establish and to enforce for all players alike. You must be consistent in this area. Basketball is a team game. Treat it as such in the area of discipline. Do not form a "star" system whereby some individuals are disciplined one way, or worse, not at all, while players of lesser ability are treated more severely.

At this juncture, let me relate a good example of this practice. During one period in my high school coaching days, my teams completed two consecutive undefeated seasons with 20-0 records. During the spring following the second season, I attended a track meet near our school's campus. There, I spotted one of my junior starters and an all-star caliber player consuming alcohol with friends. The next day, I contacted him in class and requested that he report to my office after school. He complied. As he walked into my office, I asked him to close the door and sit down. I confronted him about his conduct at the track meet. He admitted it. I then informed him that I was not going to dismiss him from the team but that he would be on probation with me. The terms of the probation were as follows. When basketball practice began the next season, he would be required to practice with the team as usual. However, when the playing season began, he would not dress for games. He would sit on the bench in street clothes and support his teammates. The probation would last as long as I determined. He agreed to the punishment. He reported for practice as usual, the next season. When the regular season started, he sat on the bench. We lost the first game of that season in a double overtime by two points. Remember, we had previously won 40 consecutive games. I believe we would have won that game with this player participating. After four other games, which we won, this player was given permission to dress for games. We had another very successful season, losing only two other games.

Some years later, this player showed up at my summer pool manager's job site. We had a nice reunion. Late in the conversation, he thanked me from the bottom of his heart for the action I took during his playing days. He said, "You probably saved me from myself, and you certainly taught me a valuable life lesson."

My point: In all probability, he did not "like" me very much at the time of his probation, but he respected my decision and me, particularly in later life. I also believe the rest of his teammates respected me for my decision, even though we lost our consecutive game-winning streak. I certainly respected myself for it. As a coach, you must demand the highest standards of integrity of your players and not be reluctant to discipline when necessary. Yet, at times you must have a forgiving heart without being weak and vacillating. My own personal succinct theory was, "BE FIRM, BUT FAIR!"

Sometimes your actions will speak louder than words of a lecture. Let me illustrate. During one of my junior college seasons, my team took a two-game overnight trip to the Pittsburgh area. We played dismally and lost both games. At our motel, I inspected the players' rooms prior to me boarding the bus to return home. This was my usual practice following overnight trips. In some of the rooms, I discovered several empty beer cans. I gathered and put them in a large garbage bag, walked to our loaded bus, got on, and tossed the bag of cans down the aisle of the bus. I said nothing and sat in my usual seat at the front of the bus. When we arrived back at our college gymnasium, I instructed the team to go to our locker room and dress in their practice gear and report to the gymnasium. All obeyed and reported to the court area. One player asked, "Where are the balls, coach?" My reply, "We won't need them." I ordered them to the baseline for wind sprints. We ran for two hours. The results; I never had any more problems with beer cans in players' rooms and we won the next eight games in a row. FIRM, BUT FAIR? I believe so.

CHAPTER 3

SOME QUALIFICATIONS OF A COACH

To coach, you must have the ability to teach and to lead. Coaching is teaching. You must have the aptitude for imparting information to others, so they can connect it with efficient action. It is essential that you teach at the level of understanding, present the information in a logical sequence, and have some sense of the laws of learning. Do your research in this latter area, though I will provide some data in this chapter.

Implicit in the ability to teach is the capacity to lead. Ideally, it is to direct others toward the attainment of high standards, set goals, guide along a course of respectable citizenship, and to demand the best effort and not to accept anything less. The more productive coaches plan and prepare to coach and teach. The answers to two penetrating questions will reveal the type of practice schedule a coach will decide upon.

The first question is, "How do you intend to have your team play?" As the old cliché states, "There is more than one way to skin a cat." It is likewise with selecting a style of play for your squad. Regardless, it is necessary to determine this intention in advance. Why? There are two prominent reasons. First, analyze the age and skill level of your team. This is very important. Do not expect your players to execute schemes of play that they are physically and mentally unable to perform. Secondly, no organized procedures for drills and practice plans can be established until a definitive outline has been embraced.

The second question is, "How do you expect to accomplish your plan?" The answer to this query involves the philosophical mindset of the coach with respect to practice modes to prepare a team for the season. For example, some coaches devote most of their time to scrimmage; others spend most of their practice schedule on fundamental drills; while others use scrimmage only as a means of coordinating team movements, along with group and individual drill.

Personally, I mostly used instructional fundamental drills combined with what I will call "situational scrimmage." Percentagewise, I would estimate 70 percent use of drills and 30 percent scrimmage. Very rarely, did we choose five-on-five and merely run up and down the court. In fact, almost never was that the scenario. Usually, when we scrimmaged, it was designed to accomplish some specific purpose we had pre-taught, not just to "dribble and shoot the basketball."

Each coach should determine in advance exactly how they expect to prepare the team for each daily practice session, allowing for adjustments as needed. By exactly, I mean a written schedule with minute-by-minute breakdown of each item to be covered for the entire practice. Have this in your possession and follow this plan as closely as possible, keeping in mind the factors of time and space allotted to you for practice. This advance planning not only assures one of a well-organized practice but makes it possible to get more accomplished in the time available. I can still remember when I failed to plan well, usually my practice did not go smoothly.

When you are a coach, you are an instructor, and your team members are your students. Therefore, I believe it very necessary for the coach to have some knowledge of the laws of learning. Over the years as I have observed many in action, I have concluded these skills were either not possessed by the coach in charge or ignored. This was especially true of coaches who were not accredited teachers at the school system. These would include a part-time person hired to coach and parents who become "coaches" when their children become old enough to play at some level of organized recreation league basketball. Had these adults in charge possessed a good working knowledge of some of the laws of learning as guiding principles, I believe they would have obtained the best results in the shortest time. I will list some:

1. Players learn better if they understand the relationship of one phase of the pattern of play to another. Explain the plan and its terminology to them at the outset of the season so they may see, and hopefully grasp, the goal toward which they are striving.

2. All players must have the "will to learn." Without real desire, not much learning takes place. I often would ask myself, "Is this player coachable?" There are instances where this has to be instilled in some individual players. This is absolutely true if a player does not demonstrate a fondness for some phase of the game. Defense comes to mind immediately.

3. The whole-part plan of practice, to me, is most effective and produces the best results. Teach the whole, slowly at first, with proper terminology, and then break it down into parts in drill form.

4. Repetition is a vital necessity. You must drill your team repeatedly. If coaches fail to repeat the practice of drills and team patterns, the players not only fail to improve, but forget much of what was initially introduced. Too many coaches

take it for granted that if they mention a skill or fundamental and give it only cursory attention, the players will, through some miracle, immediately grasp it. NOT TRUE! Therefore, many coaches are notorious for unfairly criticizing their players for failing to perform a skill. In reality, they have spent truly little practice time in explaining, teaching, and drilling the fundamental skill. Blocking out for defensive rebounding is one that comes to mind quickly.

5. Learning takes place more effectively when drills are practiced repeatedly in short time segments rather than in a few long periods. Again, it is all about repetition. Expect mistakes in the beginning. Over time these errors will be minimized. Make every attempt to stick fervently to your practice schedule. Long, drawn out drills will not increase efficiency quicker. Stay within the short time frames scheduled. Repeat on following practice days as needed. Some will occur daily. Practice does make perfect, to a degree. However, it is prudent to insert "patience" to that formula.

6. It is wise to plan practices so that learning progresses with as little retrogression as

possible. I believe it is judicious to give every drill a name. The main reason for this is to save valuable time. Thusly, it will not be necessary to explain each drill in detail every time it is repeated in ensuing practices. Always attempt to repeat new drills in the next few days following their introduction. The amount of repetition thereafter will depend on the coach's ability to observe and correct obvious errors in performance, and the adeptness of the players in developing and improving. Note: Again, some drills you will use the entire season.

7. As an added suggestion, do not introduce new offensive plays or defenses on the spur of the moment, such as during a time out, at halftime or a day before a big game. If your squad has not practiced it thoroughly, do not expect the players to perform it well as a team. It is best to stick with what your team knows for certain. Good execution is what wins games, particularly in crucial situations. Go with the known!

At this juncture, I would like to mention a few suggestions about the overall seasonal practice schedule. For me, there were three stages of yearly practice. The heaviest, longest, and most strenuous was during preseason before competition began. Desire and enthusiasm are at a high level during these sessions. Plus, there is much to learn and a short time to grasp it all. Once the season begins, there should be a gradual lightening and shortening of the daily practice schedule. The third stage takes place after the competitive season is about a half to two-thirds completed. Keep practices at reduced duration during this time. Sometimes, depending on the situation, it is practical to cancel on occasion.

Here is another recommendation. Before the first practice, I believe it advisable to make two all-inclusive lists, one dealing with defense and the other for offense. Included should be all items to be discussed, taught, and drilled in each category. Then, as you encompass each item into your daily schedule, check it off. In this manner, you will not omit anything prior to you first regular season game. Of course, one or two practice sessions are not always adequate to instill the proficiency required. Therefore, drill as necessary after the season begins. With the check off method, you have at least introduced each item during the preseason.

One final helpful hint is to either save your dated daily practice schedules in a file or to write them in a notebook. They will help you prepare in future seasons. I still have most of mine.

CHAPTER 4

TERMINOLOGY

As you begin your attempts to teach basketball, I, unequivocally believe it is necessary to define the terms of the game. The sport does have its own language and definitions. I believe it is required for you as coach to explain these terms to your players. I said "explain," not merely mention in passing. Never take for granted that because you know what you mean that your players understand what you mean. Always take the time to explain and yes, demonstrate what you are trying to teach. Therefore, I am listing several defensive and offensive terms that serve as good examples. There are others, but this is a good beginning.

Defensive Terms

1. On Side (Ball Side)
Divide the court in half lengthwise. The half of the court where the ball is located is the on-side.

2. Off Side (Help Side)
That half of the court where the ball is not located.

3. Line of the Ball
When an offensive player has possession of the ball, visualize an imaginary line drawn through the ball from sideline to sideline.

4. Slide to the Ball (Jump to the Ball)
When the offensive player you are guarding with the ball passes, the defensive player must move instantly in the direction of the pass to a new defensive position. This is often called the "help" position.

5. Help
See #4 above. After the slide to the ball, the defender is now in the "help" position.

6. Help and Recover
In #5 above, if offensive player dribbles at the helper and then passes to helper's man, the helper stops dribble penetration (the help) and

recovers to re-guard his man by sliding to the ball.

7. Head on the Ball
When guarding a dribbler, position your feet and body so your head is even with the ball.

8. Overplay (Contesting)
While guarding an offensive player without the ball, position yourself so he cannot receive a pass without moving. Ideally, the defender makes the player move farther from the scoring area.

9. Deny (Front)
When guarding an offensive player anywhere on the court, do all in your power to keep the player from catching the basketball. This defensive tactic is used quite often in defending the post or pivot area. It is also employed when double-teaming or trapping the offensive player with the ball by the other three defenders.

10. Force
When guarding a dribbler or player with the ball, make (force) them to go in a certain direction or to a certain area of the court.

11. Switch
Two defenders exchange defensive assignments as offensive players cross.

12. Blitz Switch
A maneuver used to surprise an offensive dribbler. A defender forces the dribbler toward the closest defensive teammate. Once the dribbler is close enough (five or six feet), the nearby teammate will aggressively attack (blitz) the dribbler while dribbler defender switches to blitzer's man.

13. Trap (Double Team)
Once a dribbler goes to a certain area or the ball is passed to a certain area, two defenders will trap or double team the player with the ball. See # 9 above.

14. NOW! (Or any other signal word chosen)
What the defender guarding the dribbler yells loudly when dribbler picks up the ball. Defender will guard player with the ball very aggressively and closely while other teammates attempt to deny the ball to the other four offensive players.

15. Crossing the Lane
When a teammate on ball side gets beaten by a dribbler, a defensive teammate on the help side must often cross the foul lane to stop the

dribbler. Most necessary as the offensive dribbler drives the baseline.

16. Defensive Transition

The act of all five players getting back on defense to defend as quickly as possible after either scoring or losing the ball on offense. I used to call this, "The Defensive Fast Break!" See #3 above, The Line of the Ball. The objective for all five defenders is to at least get below the line of the ball.

OFFENSIVE TERMS

1. The Block
The 12″ x 8″ lane space marker along the free throw lane.

2. Run to the Block
When fast breaking, you may want certain players to sprint to the block. You may also want a post player to establish position just above the block at times. Also see #11 below.

3. "V" Cut or "L" Cut
Types of footwork maneuvers by offensive players without the ball to get open to receive a pass when overplayed by the defense.

4. Clear Out
When a teammate of the dribbler vacates the area of the court as the dribbler advances toward that area.

5. Back Door
A quick cut to the basket when overplayed by a defender.

6. Spacing
The distance between offensive players in the half-court scoring area, usually 12 to 15 feet. This is done in order to better spread the defense.

7. Middle Lane
The area of the court from baseline to baseline as wide as the free throw lane.

8. Right & Left Outside Lanes
The area of the court from baseline to baseline as wide as from sideline to near line of free throw lane.

9. Overload
Placing more offensive players in an area of the court than defenders in that area.

10. Triangle Spacing
Spacing three offensive players to create an overload or passing lanes, ideally 12 to 15 feet apart.

11. Posting Above the Block
All offensive players who are directed to post up low, must ensure their foot closest to baseline is on or above the Block. See #1 above.

12. Screen
A legal act whereby an offensive player gets in the path of a defender of a teammate. Be sure to read the rules about screening so you can teach what is legal.

13. Head Hunt
Finding the defender of a teammate for which you want to screen for in order to allow that teammate to cut to receive the ball.

14. Face the Basket
Being an offensive threat when in possession of the ball.

15. Triple Threat Position
Player with ball is poised with the ball so they can pass it, shoot it or dribble it.

16. Pass and Step In
After passing ball to a teammate, step closer to basket. Used often against zone defense.

17. A Gap (or Hole)
Space between two defenders. Usually talked about against zone defenses.

18. Offensive Transition
The act of getting to the offensive end of the court as quickly as possible after gaining possession of the ball. Particularly after a steal, interception, or defensive rebound.

19. Reversing the Ball

Passing the ball quickly on the perimeter from one side of the offense to the other. Used mostly against zone defenses.

CHAPTER 5

MY COACHING PHILOSOPHY

Before explaining my philosophy, I feel it necessary to briefly discuss some "preliminaries" concerning your coaching venue, the gymnasium. As I mentioned before, coaching is teaching. The gymnasium and the basketball court are your classroom. Your classroom must be conducive to learning. Attempt to have your gymnasium as follows:

1. Private for coaching staff. Do not allow outsiders to wander in and out at their leisure, unless invited.
2. Properly ventilated and temperature controlled.
3. As clean as possible, especially the playing floor.

4. Proper nets on all goals.
5. Adequate drinking water in the gym or nearby.
6. Easily accessible rest room facilities.
7. First aid supplies on location.

In Chapter 1, I wrote, "It is important to adopt a coaching philosophy." I did this. Allow me to list what I believed, held true and did my utmost to teach to the best of my ability.

Defensive Philosophy

1. Defense should be the most consistent phase of the team effort. Do not allow constant defensive mistakes.

2. We played multiple defenses with solid man-to-man principles as our foundation for all defenses.

3. The defense must "take charge" of the offensive opponents. Our defenses were designed, hopefully, to dictate what happens before something happens to hurt us.

4. Excellent team defense is based on five defenders thinking, reacting, anticipating,

and hustling EVERY time the opponents have possession of the ball.

5. A constant reminder: REMEMBER we are on defense the instant after we lose possession of the ball, including a successful field goal or foul shot.

6. EVERY time the ball moves on offense via a pass or dribble, ALL five of our defenders must react instantly to that action.

7. Never rest on defense! NEVER means NEVER!

8. A player will be substituted more quickly for defensive mistakes than offensive ones.

9. Unless instructed otherwise, always pressure the ball in your defensive area regardless of the type of defense.

10. NEVER allow an offensive player to cut towards the ball and catch it in the lane or post area. NEVER means NEVER.

11. Must prevent the ball from going inside our zone defense by a pass or dribble.

12. When we play zone, we will always HUSTLE! I always wanted to conjure up a different name other than zone. Why? Because there is a tendency for players to get lazy.

13. Excellent defense MUST become a habit. Play excellent defense notwithstanding of the score or time of game for the entire game of EVERY game.

14. ALL five defenders must transition from offense to defense on EVERY loss of possession as quickly as humanly possible!

15. Must be an excellent defensive rebounding team. We cannot play excellent perimeter defense and then easily allow second chance rebounding points.

Offensive Philosophy

1. Fast break at every opportunity, but under control, not "run and gun." Get a high percentage shot at the conclusion of the

break, with offensive rebounding opportunity, if needed.

2. A good shot is defined as a shot within each individual's range while open with teammates in possible rebounding position. Note: Sometimes an open shot is a bad shot depending on time and score of the game. Be aware of these.

3. Use the dribble as a weapon, that is, to advance the ball, drive to the basket, create a passing angle or to avoid, or get out of trouble. Avoid the "one bounce habit."

4. Learn to expect and how to handle the double-team.

5. A good passing team will get good shots.

6. When in possession of the ball, see the entire court in front of you and any open teammates.

7. DO NOT THROW SOFT, LOB PASSES, particularly versus presses or half-court zones. Receivers must come to the pass.

8. Various offensive patterns are team oriented. They are designed for all to

handle the ball and get their shots. This is best for the team scoring balance.

9. When forced to play 5-on-5 in the half-court, make the defense play defense with player movement and smart passing, unless a quick, high percentage is obtained. Must be an excellent offensive rebounding team. GO GET THE MISSED SHOT EVERY TIME!

10. Learn to play without the ball. Keep the defense occupied. Go "back door" or down screen if overplayed.

11. Must be interested mainly in TEAM statistics, not individual ones.

12. All players must learn to play efficiently with both hands. This includes dribbling especially as well as shooting layup shots. They must learn and improve using their "off" hand in practice drills. Hint: ALWAYS PROTECT THE BALL BY HAVING THE PLAYERS BODY BETWEEN THE BALL AND THEIR DEFENDER. With the dribble: head up and not looking at the ball. This latter skill is one they can practice on their own as well as in regular team practice sessions.

13. Team should be capable of playing at any tempo.

14. Though layup shots are high percentage ones, do not take them for granted. They are not automatic, so do not merely toss the ball on the backboard. There is no guarantee of two points. Learn proper technique and fundamentals. Practice diligently.

15. Learn to be a good foul shot shooter. Success in this area will result in a victory many times.

16. The quickest way to advance the ball is with a pass. See the whole court and pass to the open teammate ahead.

    To summarize, these lists are a good general collection of principles to form a basic philosophy of both phases of basketball. Adopt them as you see fit to meet the abilities of your players. For example, you may decide that your team is not capable of playing fast break basketball. So do not attempt it. Play at a slower pace.
    Every player on your squad may not possess the necessary quickness and agility to apply the proper pressure on the ball. Therefore, be aware of these shortcomings and adjust accordingly. However, when defending, I strongly believe that far too many coaches

decide well in advance not to use man-to-man and almost automatically play zone. I discuss this option in more detail in the next chapter.

CHAPTER 6

DEFENSE #1, OFFENSE #2

I purposely chose to emphasize defense first and offense secondarily, particularly during early practice sessions. Yes, I do realize your team must score points to win. However, I felt that defense would and should be the most consistent part of our team. I told my teams, "Whether we win 46 to 45 or 91 to 90, the end objective was to win." I believed good defense was the best first step toward accomplishing that goal. Whenever I scouted an opponent, my first concerns were defensive matchups, and what we had to do defensively to win. Defense was my creed and I put it into action in every practice session.

To strive for that winning goal, 75 percent of our initial preseason practices dealt with running drills and defensive footwork. I will explain the drills in a later chapter. We did the running drills, with balls in use, to get into good physical condition. The footwork drills were designed to aid us defensively, as well as, to get our legs in great playing shape. Remember, you do play sound, hopefully effective, defense with your feet and legs. My main objective was to lay a foundation for each player to properly perform man-to-man defense, both individually and as a team. I believe if a team masters the defensive techniques, it is much better prepared to use multiple defenses. I am thoroughly convinced if a team can play man-to-man reasonably, it will be a more skilled zone defense team or pressing squad. After all, they must have a defender guarding the offensive player with the ball in every defense. Proper individual footwork and positioning must be employed in these situations, so teach it and drill it. Be insistent and emphatic. Do not allow bad defensive habits!

Make no mistake, teaching defense is no easy task. That is why many coaches ignore it or give it cursory attention. First of all, the players do not really fully understand the importance of defense.

Most likely, no one before you has emphasized it. They like dribbling and shooting the basketball. They relish the "glory" attached to scoring points. You, as coach, must influence a change in their attitude toward this important aspect necessary for winning basketball. How can you do this? There is really no mystery, no short cuts and no magic formula; but over time you can and must do it. Here are some suggestions. Tell your team that good defensive players will play. Once you do, stick to your promise. Reward and praise exemplary defensive efforts, i.e., steals, deflections, interceptions, anticipatory movements, conspicuous hustle, and getting loose balls. The "king" of defensive efforts is "drawing the charge" against an offensive dribbler. With this play, your team gains possession of the ball. Plus, a personal foul is charged against the dribbler and a team foul against the opposition. TEACH IT! DRILL IT! Whenever one of my players succeeded in this effort, we stopped practice momentarily and all would applaud the player. Believe me, you are in business if you can have one perimeter defender and one interior defender commit to this skill on a consistent basis. We often gave an award at the end of the season to the player determined to be the best defender.

    I found the best way to alter attitudes toward defense was to constantly drill it every day. It would start on the very first drill of the very first day of practice every season. That drill was always a defensive one, usually the proper defensive stance. I will elaborate the specifics of this in another chapter. From that beginning, we continued day by day of every early season practice schedule with some man-to-man defensive fundamentals. It was like building a house, step by step, from the bottom up. As I stated in Chapter 3, some laws of learning, i.e., repetition, teach and re-teach, drill and re-drill, review, and repeat, teach the whole and then the parts, are all significant in this process. I staunchly believe this set the tone that our team was going to play defense! We did not just talk about it, we PRACTICED it zealously every day. We taught it! We drilled it! We helped each other! We worked hard and took pride in it! Did we improve? You bet we did! Every season, slowly, but methodically, I could sense and see a change of attitude toward defense by our players. It did not always happen quickly, or even peacefully for some. It was always a process, day by day, drill by drill. It never occurred easily. It was work, but eventually the team bought into the work ethic and took immense pride in the results. This was especially true once the season started and we began winning. They were able to see the results of their hard work, grit, and determination. "SEEING WAS BELIEVING." As an added note, we always broke every team huddle with either a "HARD WORK" or "DEFENSE"' yell.

I would like to illustrate at this point why a team's defensive ability should be measured by the differential between points scored and points allowed. Some teams are high scoring ones. Some teams use ball control and methodical patterns. Naturally, if your team scores lots of points on average per game, the opponents get more possessions, and hence, more opportunities to score. I specifically remember one high school season when my team was only permitting 45 points per game, and no one had scored 50 or more on us. Late in the season, we played and won 103 to 56. After the game, the opposing coach bragged to me about scoring over 50 points. My answer to him was, "Yes, but we scored over 100 and you certainly got a lot more offensive chances, and I played my entire bench." My point is, just because you only allow a low number of points per game does not make you necessarily a good defensive team. One team may score 58 points per game and allow 48 per game, a 10-point differential. Another team may score 72 points per game and allow 55 per game, a 17-point differential. To me, the latter is the better defensive team, even though they permit more points per game.

To summarize, sell defense, practice defense, and reward defensive efforts. The price is dedication by the coaching staff and, most of all, by the players. No, Rome was not built in a day. Neither was a good defensive basketball team. Be patient and consistent as it does take hours and hours. If your practice time is limited, keep your defenses simple and low in number. Teach the bare fundamentals. However, please do not use the time factor as an excuse for not spending necessary effort to teach man-to-man defense. LOSERS ALIBI! WINNERS WORK! WINNERS DO WHAT LOSERS NEGLECT!

CHAPTER 7

INDIVIDUAL MAN-TO-MAN DEFENSIVE FOOTWORK FUNDAMENTALS

There are two phases of man-to-man defense. They are guarding the player with the ball, and the total 5-on-5 team defense.

As I mentioned in Chapter 6, the very first drill we practiced, after warm-ups, was the proper stance for the man-to-man technique. Here is a complete description of that stance. I hereby give credit to Morgan Wootten, former renown coach at DeMatha High School in Hyattsville, Maryland for this and other information in this chapter.

1. The Man-to-Man Defensive Stance – Head to Feet.

2. Head - Up and directly in the middle of the shoulders.
3. Eyes - Looking straight ahead.
4. Shoulders - Parallel to the floor and over the balls of the feet.
5. Back - Fairly straight with no more than 45-degree angle to floor.
6. Chest - Facing the opponent, NOT THE FLOOR!
7. Waist - NOT BENT!
8. Buttocks - Low as possible and in a squat position.
9. Thighs - Fairly tight and in a 45-degree angle to floor.
10. Knees - BENT! Body is lowered by bending knees, not waist.
11. Feet - Slightly wider than shoulders and weight equally distributed on balls of both feet. One foot forward and one foot back. Toes of back foot about equal with heel of front foot. Point toes of back foot at 45-degree angle away from front foot.
12. Hands - Palms up at knee level, but inside the knees.
13. Elbows - Slightly bent.

In my experience, the stance came sort of "natural" for some players, while it was a little awkward for others. The most common mistake was bending at the waist to lower the body. This put their head in front of their feet instead of over them. It would be exceedingly difficult to retreat step from this position. It would also cause the chest to face the floor. Players do not like to bend their knees to lower their upper body. Why? Because when done properly, they really feel the strain in their thighs. They take the easy way out by keeping their knees straight and bending at the waist. This also makes their backs more parallel to the floor and hides their chest. As a coach facing the player, you should see the numbers or lettering on their practice jerseys.

There are four directions in which a defensive player must be able to move efficiently. They are:
1. Backwards -------- Retreat step
2. Forwards ---------- Advance step
3. Right ---------------- Slide step
4. Left ------------------ Slide step

A fifth step, the swing step, is used to change direction and retreat on the move. This step is described below in detail. Here are some points of emphasis when moving the feet in each direction.

1. Retreat Step (This is the most difficult to perform)
   A. Pressure on toes of front foot
   B. Push front foot into the floor and shove. At the same time, take a slide step backwards with rear foot.
   C. Never bring feet any closer together than shoulder width.
   D. Do not lift back foot. SLIDE IT.

2. Advance Step

A. Push with rear foot.
B. Slide front foot forward.
C. Keep feet apart.
D. Get extra low by bending knees and lowering the buttocks. This aids when you have to retreat quickly.

3. Slide Step — Right & Left
   A. Lead with foot closest to the direction you want to move.
   B. Push off with opposite foot.
   C. NEVER BRING FEET TOGETHER! Keep feet shoulder width apart.
   D. While sliding, DO NOT BOUNCE OR BOB UP & DOWN. Keep head, shoulders, and buttocks in the same plane. MOVE THE FEET!! Coaching hint: Tell players to pretend there is a rope attached to a wall of the gym that goes through their ears and is then attached to the other wall. In effect, they slide along that rope. When they bob up & down, they are much less efficient.

4. Swing Step
   A. First movement is a quick retreat step.
   B. Then swing body and front foot to a position that now makes front foot the back foot.

C. Be careful not to open up or swing too far. Always try to keep your back and buttocks parallel to the baseline.

In summation, here are some of the most important individual man-to-man fundamentals to remember and emphasize.
1. Get low to the floor by bending the knees, not at the waist.
2. Always keep the feet apart and on the floor as much as possible.
3. The foot that moves first is the one closest to the direction in which you want to move as indicated below.
   - Advance -------------------- Front foot first
   - Retreat ---------------------- Rear foot first
   - Slide right ------------------ Right foot first
   - Slide left -------------------- Left foot first
   - Swing ------------------ Back foot first, then swing
4. Keep head and your upper body up and over the feet and buttocks. Chest should not face the floor.
5. When slide stepping, do not bounce, or bob up and down.
6. Keep the back and buttocks as square (parallel) to the baseline as much as possible.
7. Play defense by bending the knees and moving your feet, not by reaching with hands and arms.

REMEMBER: A GOOD DEFENDER WILL ALWAYS PLAY!

Now to inform you how to break down and teach this fundamental footwork. Start first with the basic stationary stance.

Spread out all the players on the court facing you. Demonstrate a proper defensive stance. Name the drill as I have suggested. Call it "STANCE" drill. Your first instruction is to tell the players which foot is the forward foot, right or left. Then yell loudly, "STANCE!" On this command, the players immediately assume a good defensive stance. Have them hold this position until you and your assistant, if available, check all stances and make corrections. Do not allow anyone to relax and stand up straight until you command them to do so. Once they relax, they are to assume the stance each time you yell, "STANCE!" Do not hesitate to have the players remain in the stance as long as you see fit. Great for the legs and thighs. As you are making corrections, have them alternate between right foot forward and left foot forward. Another technique is to have the players, while in their stance, slowly bend their knees to touch their palms to the floor between their feet. During this maneuver, check to see that you can see everyone's chest, all heads are up, and eyes front. Then, have them return slowly to proper position and hold it. Remember the thighs are at 45-degrees to the floor in a proper stance. Repeat as you desire. NEVER LET ANYONE relax until you command it. Begin your practice with this drill the very first day. Continue for at least a week. Make corrections every day.

Once you feel comfortable with the stance drill, begin to move the players. You can introduce movement the first day after the week-long stance drill. Remember, defensive players must learn to move in four different directions; forward, backward, right, and left. The backwards, or retreat step, is the most difficult. Often, I would introduce it early to get more practice for it. However, you can begin with any of the four as you determine. Then, introduce each one, day by day, and practice individually and in combination. With every drill, you are emphasizing the points of proper fundamental execution that I elaborated earlier on in this chapter. Drill them, but then drill correctly! Do not practice bad habits. Insist on proper execution. Some players will learn quicker than others. That is normal. Push hard to get all to conform and hopefully improve.

Once you have introduced all four directions plus the swing step, and have drilled daily singly and in combination, here is the next procedure. Introduce the "WAVE-FREEZE" drill. Here is its description. Spread the players out as you did in the stance drill.

Get them to assume the defensive stance with your "STANCE" command, with either right or left foot forward as you direct.

Once they are in stance, you will use your right arm to point in the direction you want the players to move; i.e., forward, back, right or left. As you direct them with a wave in the various directions, holler,

"FREEZE." This is the signal for all players to immediately stop and freeze in position. You now check their stances as to position of feet, torso, buttocks, knee bend, etc. Remember, as they change directions from right to left or left to right, a swing step in involved. This will necessitate a change as to which foot is now forward, the right or the left. EVERY TIME you yell "FREEZE" check the fundamentals I have described. In the beginning, players will make multiple mistakes. These include wrong foot forward, feet too close together, buttocks not parallel to the baseline, and improper alignment of the back feet to the front feet. Perfection is exceedingly difficult to achieve in a few players, let alone all. However, you must continually strive for it. You will be amazed how fast most of your players improve if you insist, correct, repeat, and repeat.

After you have drilled the "WAVE-FREEZE," present the "BOX" drill. In this drill, the players will perform all footwork directions on their own. You command them into a stance position, with either right or left foot forward. The players will, on your command of "GO" or blowing of a whistle, take two advance steps two retreat steps, swing, slide two steps, advance two steps, retreat two steps, swing, two slide steps, advance two steps, retreat two steps, swing, slide two steps, advance, retreat, swing, slide, advance, retreat, swing, slide, advance, retreat, swing. It is two up, two back, swing, two slides, two up, two back, swing, two slides. Thus, the box is formed. As the players execute this drill, coaches should carefully scrutinize their footwork, quickness, and fundamentals. Insist that players move as quickly as possible without being sloppy. This is a necessity to good defense. The players continue until you blow the whistle or yell "stop." Again, I repeat, do not permit laziness, sluggish moves, and poor fundamentals. Practice sound habits! As the leader be enthusiastic, energized, and upbeat in all these drills. Be snappy. Praise the good and correct the incorrect. Do not allow anyone to loaf. NOT PERMITTED ON DEFENSE!

You may ask, "How long and how often do you schedule these drills?" The answer is a definitive one. Begin the season, day one, with the stance drill for at least a week. You may start out with thirty minutes the first day and gradually reduce to five minutes at the end of the week. Depending on the progress and experience of your squad, gradually introduce the footwork directions along the way. For example, schedule stance to advance, stance to retreat, stance to advance and swing, stance to retreat and swing, stance to advance and swing and slide, stance to retreat and swing and slide. What you are accomplishing here is the breakdown of the "box" drill. Then proceed to the "Box" drill. Allow at least two weeks for this progression. Again, start EVERY practice with these drills during the two weeks. No shooting! No dribbling! Balls on the Rack! This sets the tone for DEFENSE.

The next drill to introduce is the "ZIGZAG." This is a drill to teach players how to guard an opponent dribbling the basketball.

One of the better techniques is as follows: a good defensive stance with the "head on or even with the ball" (see defensive definitions) and with solid pressure by the defender. This pressure defined as an arm's length from the dribbler. Set up the drill by splitting the court lengthwise. Space out cones, chairs or any other objects available as the dividers. Then split the squad into two groups. To begin, one player is a defender while another is the dribbler. At half speed, the dribbler will move right or left to advance the ball up court while going in a zigzag direction. The defender, with hands behind their back, assumes a proper defensive stance and slide steps in order to get the head even with the bouncing ball. The pair continue until the dribbler runs out of space at the sidelines or center court. The dribbler changes direction to proceed in the other. The defender at this point swing steps, slide steps quickly to get their head even with the ball once again and progresses with the dribbler. To repeat, the dribbler is going at half speed in the early phase of the drill. This one-on-one continues the length of the court to the far baseline. Once a twosome has reached half-court, another dribbler and defender start performing the same action. Once all twosomes reach the far baseline, the dribbler and defender switch assignments and proceed back to the original starting point. In the early going, do not let the dribbler try to beat the defender or the defender reach for the ball. The main emphasis is to make the defenders get proper positioning with footwork and keeping their buttocks parallel to the baseline behind them. You will find that a common mistake is caused when the defender swing steps as the dribbler changes direction. It is because the defender swings and opens too far, failing to square-up when they proceed to slide.

You will build on this drill day by day by allowing the dribbler to increase his speed and change direction often. The final phase is to play one-on-one at full speed. Tell the defenders that their job is not to steal the ball, but to keep the dribbler in front of them with constant pressure. If the defender is beaten, they must sprint to catch up, and ideally, to get in front of the dribbler, or at least deflect the ball from behind.

To compress this chapter, think of building that foundation for the next chapter, team man-to-man defense. It is basically a five-step process, i.e., STANCE, DIRECTONAL MOVEMENTS, WAVE-FREEZE, BOX, and ZIGZAG drills. It may appear to be a lot of information and much to learn. In part, I would agree. However, let me add, once you get involved in the various skills, the totality of it all seems to fall easily into place. Do not get trapped into feeling that all this must be accomplished in a comparative short time span. You are breaking down the WHOLE and teaching the PARTS, as I described in Chapter 3. If there is a secret, it is that you must spend practice time on some facet of individual man-to-man defense in every practice for most of the season. Schedule it, Drill it!! It is a job that is never done! Yes, it is something a portion of your team probably will not enjoy as much as offensive drills, but the end results of your diligence will eventually change their attitudes. As you move forward and your players get better, gradually shorten the duration of drills. It is even a good policy to review the essentials ever so often. It is all in your hands as to how, how much, how long, when, why, and if. Be an excellent leader, teacher, and coach. TEACH DEFENSE!

CHAPTER 8

TEAM MAN-TO-MAN DEFENSIVE FUNDAMENTALS

Following individual man-to-man fundamentals, you must teach team man-to-man defensive basics. Usually, for me, I started this scheme with the "SLIDE TO THE BALL" drill. Familiarize yourself with terms #4 and #5, slide to the ball, and help definitions in Chapter 4. Form two lines about the width of the foul lane facing the basket. Designate the first player in each line as the defender, and the second one on offense. One of the offensive players has a ball. To begin the drill, the player with the ball passes to their teammate and remains stationary. The moment they do this, their defender must instantly slide in the direction of the pass to a new defensive position. This new position is often called the "HELP" for the defender now guarding the new receiver of the pass. Once this receiver gets the ball, they hold it until the defenders move, then they return the pass back to the original passer. The defenders now reverse roles. Defender of passer slides to help, while the helper slides to defend the new receiver. Repeat this several times. Then allow the passers to become defenders and defenders go to the end of the line.

Remember to emphasize good footwork and quickness. The instant the ball leaves the passer's hands, both defenders should ideally react at that moment, not after the pass is caught. Do your utmost to get this result with each pass. Why? Because it teaches good defensive intensity, attention to the task at hand, and an attempt to take control of the offense. Review Chapter 5, defensive philosophy, item #3 which says, "take charge of the offense." To me, it is crucial in the ZIGZAG drill and here in the first team defensive drill. Insist on it. Another coaching point, be sure the help defender can always see the ball and their assigned opponent without putting their head on a swivel. Therefore, do not allow the defender to turn their back to the player they are guarding. Ideally, they should keep their posterior parallel to the baseline so they can see the ball and their opponent. A common mistake occurs on defense when the help defender performs poor footwork, often merely caused because of over hustle. This is why you must insist on proper footwork in the individual footwork drills. Repeat them often.

The next step is "HELP AND RECOVER." See Chapter 5 for definition. Use the same drill formation as described in the slide to the ball drill. However, make this addition. When the ball is passed to a receiver and the help defender makes their defensive slide toward the ball, allow the receiver to dribble drive at the help defender. Once the dribbler is stopped, they pass to their teammate. Help defender now must recover to guard this new receiver. Thus, results in help and recover. This is not easy to perform correctly. One common mistake is for the helper to reach to stop the dribbler. Thus, often fouling, instead of moving feet to get into proper stop position. The other frequent error is on the recover move. The defender often rushes directly at the new receiver, hence, becoming very susceptible of getting beaten with a quick dribble. Make the recover helper slide "over" and then "up" towards the opponent with the ball to prevent this. Repeat as needed. Then the defenders go to the end of the line and passers become defenders.

The next progression is to teach the "SHELL" or "HORSESHOE" drill. This is a 4-on-4, two guards and two forwards, perimeter set-up in the offensive half-court area. The main purpose of this drill is to instruct all four defensive players to react to a correct floor position in relation to the location of the basketball and the opponent they are responsible for guarding. Remember, in ideal team defense, every time the ball is passed in this drill, all four defenders must react instantly to the new location of the ball. I repeat, ALL FOUR!

Review the definitions in Chapter 4 of ball side and help side, because in this drill, two defenders are on the help side and two are on the ball side. Also, you must take into consideration what your defensive philosophy is as to which passes you will allow without defensive denial and which ones you will not permit without defensive pressure. This philosophy will determine how your defenders react. Personally, I always allowed the forward to guard pass and the guard-to-guard pass. My reasoning for this was to prevent dribble penetration. Therefore, I always wanted a defender in the help position. Plus, these types of passes were not going towards the basket area. Unless instructed not to, we always tried to deny the guard to forward pass at least enough to force the offensive forward to have to move away from the basket in order to receive a pass. I will discuss post defense in Chapter 14.

Start the ball with one of the forwards, O1. The positions of the four defenders should be as follows. D1 should pressure O1 and favor the baseline so O1 cannot dribble drive there. D2 should drop down toward D1 in the help position, seeing both the ball and O2. D3 slides into the foul lane where they can see both the ball and O3 without turning their head. They are now two passes away from the ball and on the help side. D4, now three passes away, moves into the foul lane even with the basket rim, where they can see both the ball and O4. In these positions, the ball side defenders are keyed to stop dribble penetration. The help side defenders, D3 and D4, are primed to prevent their assigned opponent from cutting to receive a pass without denial. Also, to help if dribble penetration to the basket area occurs.

Now start ball movement with O1 passing to O2, who holds the ball. Note: do this in the early process of learning the drill. Speed up the ball movement as increased learning takes place. As this first pass is completed, all four defenders must react, ideally at once and in unison. D2 immediately moves with advance slides to pressure O2. D1, still on ball side, slides to deny a return pass to O1. D3 slides into help position for D2 as in the help and recover drill. D4 is now two passes away and slides from out of the lane towards O4. O2 now passes to O3, who holds the ball. D3 must slide over and up to O3, as practiced in help & recover, and pressures the ball. D2 slides to help position for D3. D1, now two passes away from the ball, loosens their position from O1 towards the lane. They are now on the help side with D2. D4, now one pass away from O4, uses advance slides to deny easy pass to O4. O3 now passes to O4. Note: for drill purposes, allow this guard to forward pass. Once completed, D4 slides to pressure the ball and prevent the baseline drive by O4. D3 slides toward O4 in a help position. D2 should slide into the lane, where they can see O4 with the ball and O2 without head swivel. D1 slides into the lane even with basket rim, where they can see both the ball and O1. Once the ball has been passed around the perimeter from O1 to O2 to O3 to

O4, reverse the process and repeat in the opposite direction. Repeat several times. Then switch guards to forwards and forwards to guards so they learn defensive responsibilities from those areas of the court.

After repetitions, switch offense to defense, and then repeat as outlined above. As with all new drills, go slowly at first, correct mistakes, encourage all, and be upbeat. Always remember that a good defensive team is one where ALL players react at the instant the offensive ball position changes, either by dribble or pass.

Review the definition of "crossing the lane" in Chapter 4. If D4 gets beaten, D1, who has dropped off their assigned offensive player as far as the basket area, must cross the lane and stop O4's drive. Be sure that D1 advances as far as the block to accomplish this. Remaining under the basket will not get the job done! The other defenders rotate as follows: D4 follows dribbler and double teams with D1, D2 drops down to opposite block area to prevent a pass from O4 to O1 cutting to the basket; D3 parallels the drive by O1 into the lane to prevent a possible pass.

To drill these defensive maneuvers, allow O1 and O4 to receive a pass rather than deny it. Then permit both D1 and D4 to let O1 and O4 to drive the baseline. Also, it is necessary to change the positions of D1 through D4 so they learn the rotation and slides from all four defensive areas.

To continue the drill once O1 is stopped by D4, O1 passes out to O2 on the perimeter. All four defenders must then scramble to go "home" in relation to whom they are assigned to defend and the position of the ball. This results in D1 staying with O1 to deny, D2 slides out to O2 to pressure the ball, D3 slides to help position for D2, and D4 remains even with the basket. The ball is then passed to O3 and then to O4, and all defenders adjust accordingly. O4 is permitted to drive the baseline. D1 crosses the lane to stop O4. D4 follows dribbler and double teams with D1. D2 drops down to opposite block and D3 parallels the drive. O4 passes out to O3 and the process is repeated.

The next progression is to allow O2 or O3 to pass to O1 or O4 anytime in the above sequence, then cut hard for a possible return pass in a "give & go" maneuver. It is the responsibility of D2 or D3 to "jump to the ball" as the pass is thrown to prevent the return pass to the cutter. For drill purposes, O1 or O4 does not return the pass. The cutter, O2 or O3, will continue past the basket and proceed to the opposite corner. Meanwhile, the cutter's defender stays with the cutter until the cutter crosses the lane and is going away from the ball. The defender STOPS even with the basket, opens up so to see both the ball and their teammate, and becomes a help side defender as their teammate is now three passes away from the ball. The sequence is O2 passes to O1, and cuts to basket. O3 rotates to O2 position, O4 rotates to O3 position, and O2 cuts through to O4 position. This changes three defenders' positions, D2, D3, and D4 as they move with their assign players. In the beginning of teaching this, do so slowly and methodically to be sure all defenders are making the proper slides. Again, emphasize to all defenders not guarding the ball, particularly on the help side, that they establish their new position to be able to see both the ball and their assigned player without constantly turning their heads.

At this point, let me explain the defensive triangle principle. When an imaginary line is drawn from the ball to the defender's player, the help side defender should position himself off of that line in order to see both the ball and their player without a head swivel.

As O1 has the ball, D3 and D4 help the side defenders. The three players must establish a defensive triangle. If these defenders stand on or too close to the imaginary line to the ball, it will be necessary for them to constantly turn their heads in order to see both the ball and their assigned player. Good defense dictates that all defenders must see both without head turning. Therefore, teach defenders to form a triangle by getting off the imaginary line. How far? The flatter the triangle the better as long as they can see both the player and ball. This is not as simple as it sounds for many defenders. That is why it is best to proceed slowly at the outset to check all and correct as needed.

Now to continue the drill of the pass and cut maneuver, O1 passes back to O3, who has rotated over to fill the vacancy created by O2's pass and cut. On this pass, all defenders must make their proper defensive slides in relation to the ball and their assigned player as described earlier. O3 holds the ball momentarily and then passes to O4, who has rotated to O3's previous spot. All defenders must adjust to the new position of the ball. O4 holds the ball momentarily and then passes to O2, who has replaced O4. Note:

D2 allows the pass for drill purposes. O4 then cuts to basket as if to receive a give and go return pass. O2 does not return the pass, so O4 continues his cut to basket, crosses the lane to opposite corner to replace O1, who rotated up to replace O3. After O4 cuts, O3 moves over to replace O4. O2 now passes back to O3. All defenders have to adjust to this pass.

Once you feel your players are grasping the above necessary slides for above offensive maneuver, do this. Once O3 receives the pass from O2, give O3 a choice; return the pass to O2 and cut to basket, or pass to O1. O1 now has a choice; pass to O4 and cut through or return the pass back to O3. Call this drill "SHELL with CUTTER THROUGH." Again, start slow and do not move the ball too fast. Allow defenders to adjust on each pass and increase tempo gradually as there is a lot to comprehend here. Insert this drill into your practice schedule daily. Teach! Be demanding, but be patient!!

A helpful hint: As a coach, I believe the ideal spot to teach any of the "SHELL" drills is for you to position yourself outside of the baseline underneath the basket. From there, you can best see all the defenders, their respective movements, and reactions on every pass by the offense. Also, be sure all players perform as defenders at all four perimeter areas of the half-court.

The next logical step to teach is what could be named, "DRIVE THE GAP." It is taught to prevent dribble penetration by the offense. The setup is the same as in any part of the shell drills. Start the ball with any offensive player on the perimeter. Tell the offensive players to dribble drive into each gap of the defense and to then pass out to nearest offensive teammate when stopped. Repeat around the perimeter. The defenders must help and recover when a gap is driven, and a pass out occurs.

Another sequence is to have the offside offensive players, either O3 or O4, cut to receive a pass from O1. The defenders, either D3 or D4, must deny the pass. If O3 cuts and is denied, they curl to the opposite corner to replace O4, who rotates to O3's spot. If O4 is denied, they retreat to their original spot. After a denial, O1 passes to O2, O2 passes to O3, who then passes to O4. When O4 receives the pass, O2 or O1 cuts to receive a pass. D2 or D1 must deny the pass. This part of the shell drill emphasizes that a defender NEVER allows his player to cut towards the ball and receive a pass in the lane or post areas.

Yes, I agree, as you have read through these variations and sequences of man-to-man team defensive drills, it all sounds somewhat complicated and time-consuming. Depending on the skill level of your players and the amount of practice time available to you, pick and choose accordingly. Again, as I say to all, "Do not neglect entirely man-to-man defense." Teach as much and as quickly as your players can digest each segment. Teach and review, teach and review! Once you have incorporated man-to-man principles in your practice schedule, include some portion, no matter how limited, every practice session.

Maintain your stress on your defensive objectives. Practice, Practice, Practice! Drill, Drill, Drill!

CHAPTER 9

MAN-TO-MAN POST DEFENSE

It was always my defensive philosophy to guard the post or pivot offensive player according to how important they were to the opponent's offensive scheme. If they were the best, or nearly so, offensive player, we defended them differently than if they were not that essential to our foe's attack. For instance, if the post player rarely received the ball, we "cheated" defensively. That is to state, we did not closely guard or deny him, except to block out on rebounds. Thus, our defender assigned to the post could practically play a one-man zone, or helper type defense, when needed. However, if the post player was a terrific offensive threat, we would do all in our power to deny them access to the ball, or double team them if we failed in our attempts to accomplish that goal. We did not often "front" the post because of defensive rebounding responsibilities.

With the above philosophy stated, here are some general ways to defense post players. There are three possible areas of post defense along the lane: low, mid, or side and high. The most dangerous is the low post. I often said to my players, "When we allow an offensive player to easily catch the ball in the low post, usually something bad will happen; that being an easy score, a foul on an attempt to score or both." Therefore, we worked diligently to deny this pass because "an ounce of prevention is worth a pound of cure!" How do you do this? Here are some ways to try.

When the ball is below the foul line extended, the post defender must position themselves on the baseline side of the post player, with a hand across and up to deny a pass. In other words, play defensively on the side of the post, NOT BEHIND. Often, the defender has to "fight" for this location without fouling. If the post does receive a pass and they are a talented offensive player, double team with the defender of the player who threw the pass. Make the offense "hurt" you another way. Take away their post option by either a denial or a double team.

If the ball is above the foul line extended, defense the low post on the ball side with a hand up and across to deny a pass. Often the ball is either dribbled or passed to an area below the foul lane. When this occurs, the post defender must use quick footwork to step across in front of post and then to baseline side. Do not go behind! Move from side to front to side.

Use these same defensive principles if post is at the mid or side location. If the player is at the high post, you might choose to play behind, favoring the ball side. If you want to deny a pass to a high post player, you can either have his defender do it, or have an offside defender front the post. If you decide on the latter, have the post defender play behind.

Here is a summarized version of guarding post players up until this point.

1. Decide how important the offensive post is to the overall scheme of attack.
   a. If they are pivotal, deny any easy pass to them. Double team with the defender of the passer if post does receive a pass.
   b. If they are incidental to the offense and sort of only a fifth player, defense them loosely and have their defender be of help in the lane area to other teammates.

2. There are three possible positions for the offensive post player to locate along the lane area: low, side, or mid and high. Low is the most perilous to the defense.
   a. When the ball is located below the foul line extended, guard the post areas as follows.
      i. When low and mid, play on baseline side of post and deny.
      ii. When high, play behind post and favor the ball side.

b. When the ball is located above the foul line extended, guard the areas as follows.
   i. Low and mid, play on the ball side and deny.
   ii. High, play behind and favor the ball side.
   iii. If ball is dribbled or passed to an area below the foul line extended; post defenders must adapt. See 2a.

I would like to suggest some helpful advice concerning post players. Particularly those at the lower rung of ability and levels of competition. The majority of them are "dominant-handed." To explain, if right-handed, they will mostly use their right hand to shoot or dribble. If a lefty, they will utilize it. Therefore, teach and make sure your post defender forces their opponent to their "weak" side. In a crucial game or situation, be certain to remind them of this strategy.

Another consistent fault of post defender is to get in foul trouble by attempting to block shots, or to reach over the opponent's body to deny a pass. Concerning the shot blocking, teach your defenders not to "slap the air" or swing downward in their attempt. First of all, unless the defender has a reasonable height advantage, they will rarely be successful in blocking shots. Teach them to jump vertically with their hand or hands on a straight plane above their heads to alter a shot attempt. If unsuccessful, emphasize blocking out for rebounding.

As far as attempting to deny a pass to a post player, "an ounce of prevention is worth a pound of cure" in this situation. The defender must always, if you want passes denied, fight for proper position to get the job done. The defender must be alert at all times to beat a post player to the spot on the lane they desire. If the offensive player is beaten to the desired spot, they must either find another one or move farther from the basket. Deny them the spot and this will aid you in accomplishing your objective.

Here is further elaboration on this final point. Do not allow your post defenders to always retreat down the center of the court during defensive transition to an area in the lane under the basket. It is amazing how conditioned to doing this they become if you allow it. Where is the offensive post player going to post up? Certainly not IN THE FOUL LANE, but on the perimeter of the lane. Let us say for illustration, the offensive post player always posts up at the low block on the right or left side of the basket, depending on the position of the advancement of the ball up court. Common sense says, instruct you defenders to beat the opponent to that spot. If the defender does not, the offensive post gets to their favorite spot easier, receives the pass, and the defense is immediately in trouble. Do not allow this! That is the ounce of prevention. Naturally, you will not be successful all the time, but every bit helps. Drill It! Emphasize It! Practice It! Make the habit a good one.

CHAPTER 10

EARLY SEASON PRACTICE DRILLLS

As I mentioned in Chapter 6, 75 percent of our early preseason training included defensive footwork and running drills.

I have detailed the defensive work. Now I will describe some of the full court running drills, with a ball and shooting included, that our players seemed to enjoy. My main objectives were to have extensive running for conditioning purposes, while simultaneously practicing ball handling, dribbling, passing, and catching on the move, and shooting layups. As was my custom, I named each drill. These included "DRIBBLE & CHASE," "MUST MAKE," "6 PASS," "3 PASS," "CONTINUOUS 2-ON-1," and "11 MAN." They are diagramed #1 through #6 with explanation for each.

In all these drills, you must emphasize good passing, dribbling and shooting with proper hand, making layups, and most of all, running at full speed under control. I believe the sheer drudgery of running is somewhat eliminated or reduced for the players with these types of drills. Since they have a ball and can pass, dribble and shoot, they tend to forget how much and how long they are running. Thus, they do not loaf or "save themselves" as much as they tend to do when merely running wind sprint drills. You can still use these, if desired, at the conclusion of practice.

"Dribble & Chase" Drill

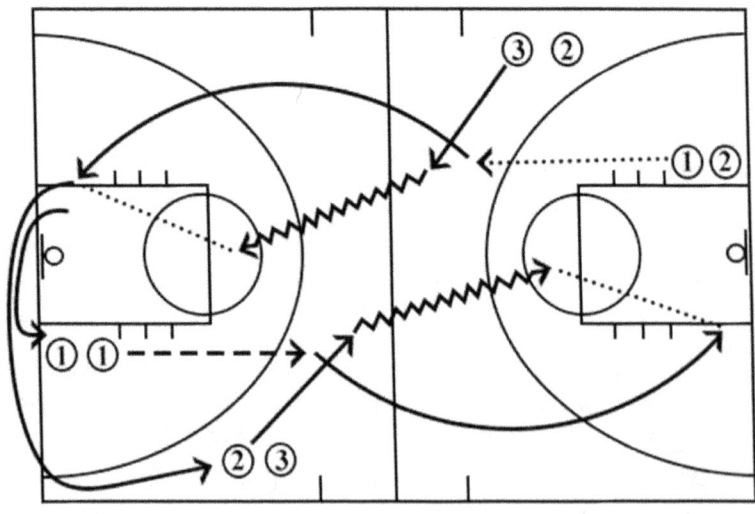

Divide the court in half lengthwise. Station four lines, two at each end of the court. One line at each end of the court will be at the block to the right of the basket and the other at the hash mark on the sidelines. The first player at the block will have a ball. When the drill begins, that player will pass to a cutting player from the line at the hash mark as they move toward the center of the court. That receiver will dribble at full speed toward the center of the foul line at the opposite end of the court. The passer will then sprint-chase to the opposite end of the court, using the right outside lane of the court, while the dribbler goes up the middle lane to the center of the foul line. The dribbler will deliver a bounce pass to the chaser as they close in on the basket for a right-handed layup shot. Simultaneously, the two lines at the other end of the court are doing likewise. In other words, there are four players in action at once with two balls; two dribblers and two chasers. Once the chaser shoots the layup, they go to the passer line at the opposite end and the dribbler goes to the line at the hash mark on the opposite side of the court. The next player in the passer line is poised to rebound the made layup and continue the drill continuously to the opposite basket. At your choice, blow the whistle and have the lines at each end switch positions; the passer-chasers to the hash mark and the dribblers to the block. Then you can repeat the drill on the left side of the court to shoot left-handed layups and dribbles.

This drill emphasizes good passing, speed dribbling, fast break sprints to the block, proper layup shooting, and alertness. This drill is continuous, and players need to be ready for their turn.

How to Coach Basketball

"Must Make" Drill

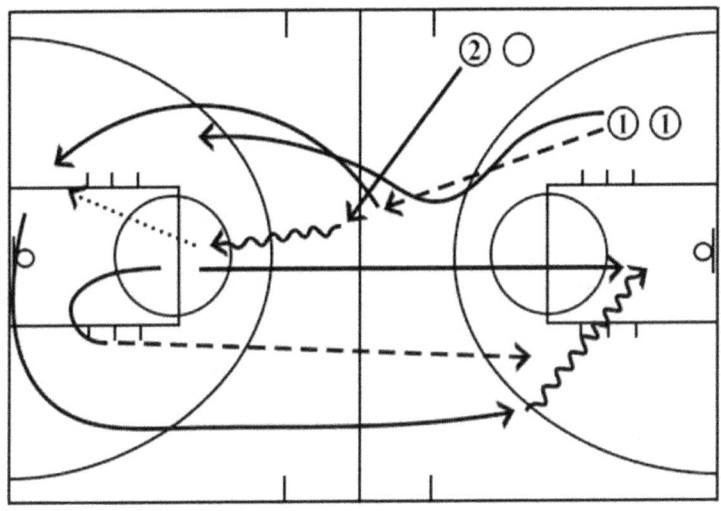

This was one of my favorite drills. Why? Because there were definite objectives to accomplish. If the players involved failed, they were required to repeat the drill while others watched. Begin the drill with two lines as in diagram #1; one line on the block with a ball and the other at the sideline hash mark. To start, the first player at the hash mark cuts hard toward the center circle to receive a pass from the player at the block. Once receiving the pass, that player dribbles hard toward the center of the foul line at the opposite basket. The passer chases the dribbler in the right outside lane as in "dribble & chase." The dribbler delivers a bounce pass to chaser for a right-hand layup shot. After the shot, the shooter immediately sprints down the court toward the opposite basket. Meanwhile, the passer rebounds the ball and immediately throws a leading baseball pass to the player sprinting down court. Upon receiving the pass, the player drives hard for the basket to MAKE a right-hand layup. This is the first of the MUST MAKE objectives. The other is for the passer to sprint up court and catch the ball as it passes through the nets before hitting the floor. If either is not successful, those same two players must repeat the drill at once while the others watch. I felt this emphasized the importance of making layups and always sprinting the length of the court regardless. At your choice, blow the whistle and have the lines switch positions; block to hash mark and hash mark to block. Likewise, to practice left-hand layups, move the lines to other side of court and repeat the drill there.

"6 Pass" Drill

How to Coach Basketball

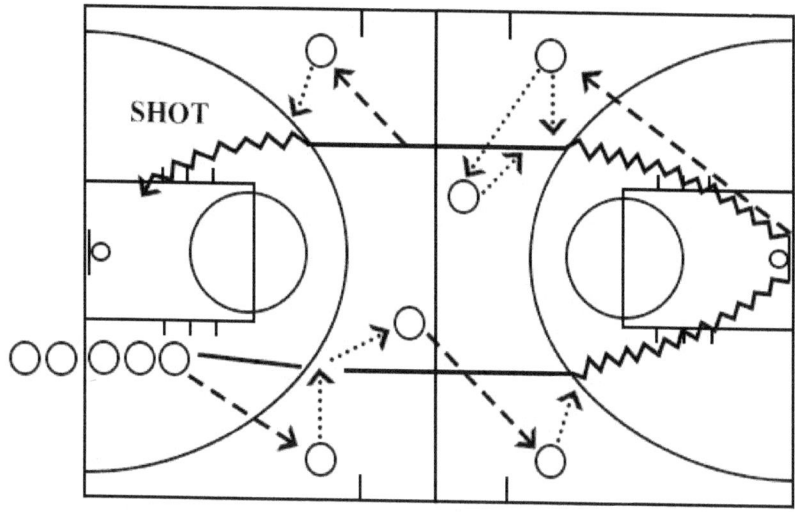

To begin, station six pass receivers, three on each side of the court; two at the foul line extended on each side, and one each on the near side of the center circle at midcourt. Have all six players face inward, so as to be in position to receive a pass and then to return the pass. The remaining players will form a line at the block near the basket. The first two players will have a ball. The first player passes their ball to a receiver at the foul line extended. The passer then sprints in a straight line between the foul line extended receiver and the receiver at center circle on the same side of the court. After catching the first pass, the receiver quickly returns the pass to the sprinting player, who then passes to the receiver at midcourt, who quickly passes back to the sprinting player, who then passes to the receiver at the other foul line extended, who returns the pass to the sprinting player, who then goes to the basket for a right-hand layup. The shooter retrieves their rebound and follows the same procedure with the three receivers on the other side of the court. Then they shoot a right-hand layup. To make the drill continuous, once the first sprinting passer gets past midcourt, have the next person with a ball begin the same path on both sides of court. Continue as you see fit, then blow the whistle and replace the six passers with six different ones and continue. Once you are satisfied, move the line on the block to the other side of the court and proceed to shoot left-hand layups.

    This drill emphasizes short crisp passes that are receivable, proper layup form, sprinting under control, catching and receiving on the move, and alertness.

"3 Pass" Drill

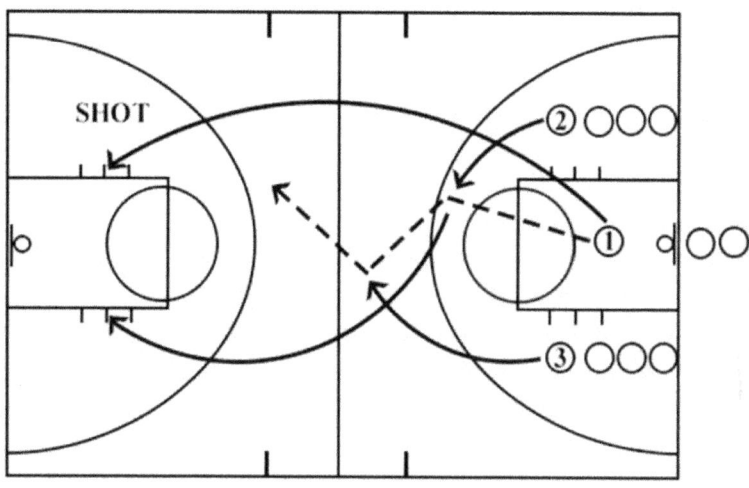

Position three lines at one end of the court. One under the basket with a ball and the other two on either side past the center of the fast break lanes. Begin by having the first person in the right lane sprint toward the center circle and receive a pass from the center line. After passing the ball, the passer sprints behind the receiver at full speed to get into the center of the outside lane. At the moment the first pass is released, the person in the left line MUST sprint down the court and angle in towards the center to get into position to receive a second pass from the first receiver on the right. The first receiver makes the second pass to that player. By this time, if the first passer from under the basket has done their job, they should be in position to receive the third pass from the outside left player and go to the basket for a right layup. If done properly, the three players should be able to progress the length of the court with three passes and no dribbles for a layup. However, it is OK if there is a dribble at the end in order to time the footwork for the layup.

To make the drill continuous, the shooter retrieves the ball after the layup, the first receiver after making the second pass proceeds to the right side of the basket, and the second passer proceeds to the left side of the basket. Now the person with the ball makes the first pass to the right and all players continue as they did from the start of the drill to the other basket for a layup. It will be necessary to rotate the lines so all players get practice from each position. Also, start with the first pass to the left to shoot left-hand layups.

This drill emphasizes fast break passes, sprinting, catching and passing on the move, proper layup form, and alertness.

"Continuous 2-on-1" Drill

How to Coach Basketball

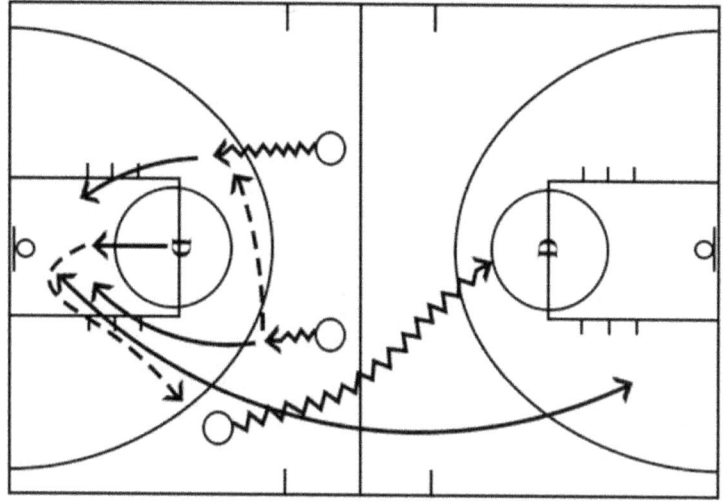

This drill is mainly an offensive one. However, you should point out the objectives of the defense before practicing this to make the offense work harder. The main objective of the defense is not to allow a layup and to make the offense make as many passes as possible. This delays the offense until the lone defender can obtain some help. Neither is possible sometimes if the offense performs well. If the offense must shoot a jump shot rather than a layup, then the defense has done an acceptable job. Another defensive technique is for the defender to "cat & mouse" the dribbler as they advance in an attempt to get the dribbler to stop or guess as to what the defender is going to do.

To set up the drill, place a defender in each foul lane at the foul line. Position a line of players to the right of each foul lane just inside of the foul line extended. To begin, put two players at midcourt, one with a ball. The two players then attack one of the baskets, ala 2-on-1. The lone defender at that basket does their best to defend as described above. Once the shot is taken, made or missed, the defender rebounds and passes out to the first player in line outside the foul lane. Then those two now attack the lone defender at the opposite basket. The first two offensive players now remain at the basket where they attempted to score. One will become the next defender at that basket and the other gets in the line outside the foul lane. The same scenario takes place at the other basket and the drill runs continuously. You may, if you choose, stop the drill at some point, and place the line outside the foul lane on the left rather than the right.

"11 Man" Drill

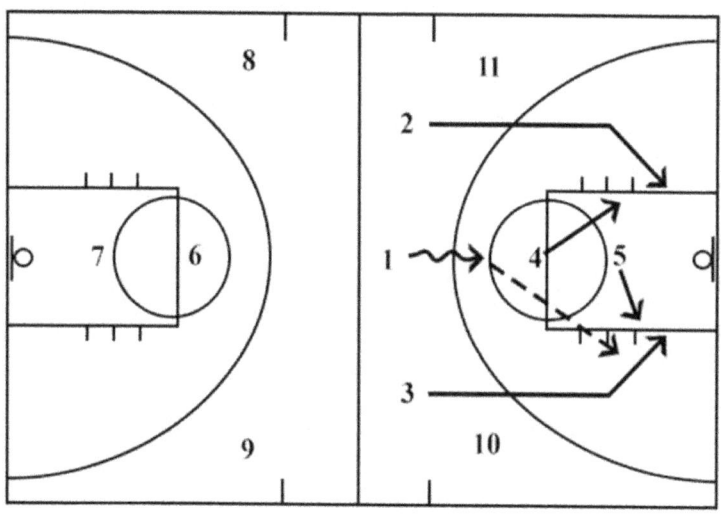

Diagram 1

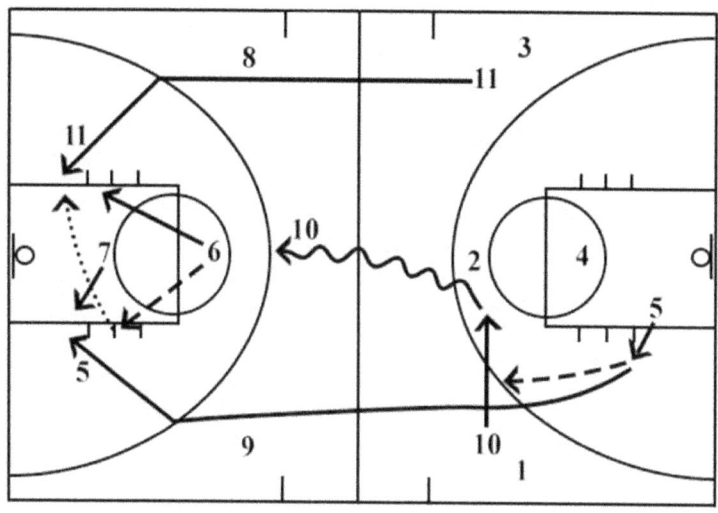

Diagram 2

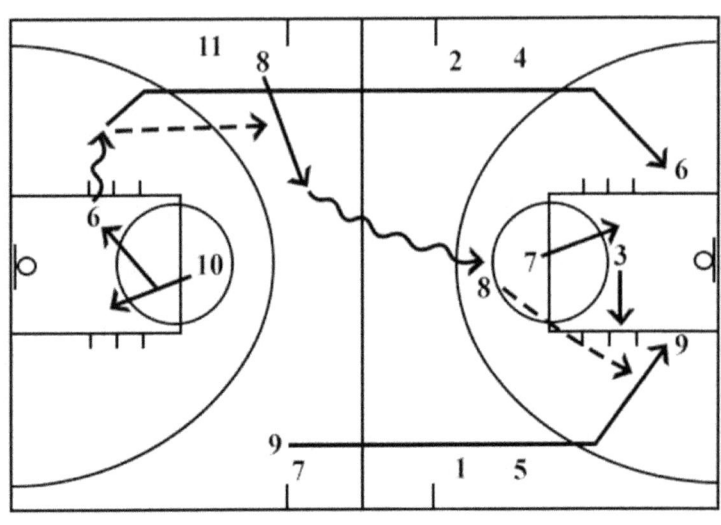

Diagram 3

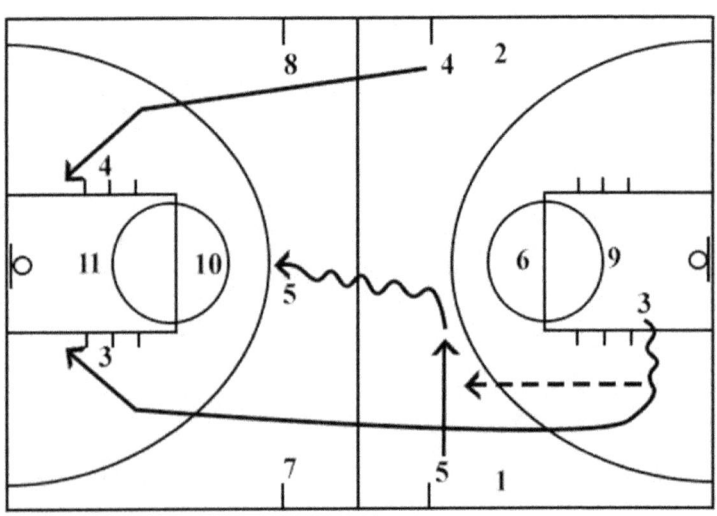

Diagram 4

Since we would attempt to be a fast break team, this is another drill I liked very much. It is mainly an offensive drill, but again it is best to demonstrate and teach how to defend against a 3-on-2 offensive attack. These defensive techniques are as follows: align two defenders in tandem in each foul lane. Place one at the foul line and the other in the center of the lane. The job of the first defender at the foul line is very similar to that of the lone defender in the 2-on-1 drill described earlier. One additional maneuver is for the player to slide to the opposite block once the offense makes a pass to the right or left of the lane. The back defender must slide to the side of the first pass by the offense. If the offense passes back toward the foul line, then the initial top defender must slide in that direction and their partner slides back into the center of the lane, as they were positioned in the beginning. Usually when this occurs, the offense takes a jump shot rather than a layup. In any case, the defense tries to make the offense attempt as many passes as possible to delay them from scoring.

This drill is called "11-man drill" because there are 11 different positions for players. After the drill starts, there is continuous action up and down the court, even on made shots, turnovers, and out-of-bounds. Here is the positioning of the players: two in tandem formation in each of the foul circles (four), one each at the foul line extended on both sides of the of the court at both baskets (four), and three spread at midcourt with one ball to begin 3-on-2 at one of the baskets. Any extra players can get in line at any of the locations outside the foul line extended areas.

To begin the drill, the player with the ball at center court and the other two on either side, attack a basket ala 3-on-2. Therefore, you now have 5 of the 11 in action. Whatever happens with the 3-on-2, like a made layup, jump shot, a missed shot or a turnover. One of two defenders in the lane will get possession of the ball. They will start a new 3-on-2 by passing to a player waiting in the foul line extended area. That player will immediately dribble to the center fast break area while the player who passed that player the ball cuts behind the receiver (just like in the 3-pass drill) and sprints toward the opposite basket. The other player on the opposite side of the court at the foul line extended now joins the other two by sprinting to the far end basket. You now have a 3-on-2 going toward that basket. While those players are attacking, the players who have just concluded a 3-on-2 will do this. One will become a defender in the foul lane and the other two will get in the foul line extended area, one on each side for balance.

In summary, you will have a continuous 3-on-2 fast break drill. In the beginning you may find it necessary to stop and re-teach who goes where, when, and how. Also, sometimes bad passing and poor ball handling will disrupt the flow of the drill. Once you have scheduled this drill enough and your players have digested it, I believe they will improve and enjoy this drill. Why? Because it is game-like, offense versus defense, and all players are intensely involved.

CHAPTER 11

SOME ZONE DEFENSIVE SUGGESTIONS

As I stated in Chapter 6, I believe it is best to teach basic man-to-man fundamentals before any other defenses of a multiple defense system. You might want to review the reasons for that statement.

When playing man-to-man defense, each defender is assigned to guard an individual opponent. It is that player's responsibility to defend that opponent wherever they move, run or cut between the black lines. The defenders can be instructed to guard intensively full court, ¾ court, ½ court or just the last third of the court, the scoring area.

On the other hand, when the defensive team decides to play scoring area zone defense, each individual defender is assigned an area of the court to defend with different slides. These slides are determined by the alignment of the defense and the different locations of the ball as it is passed or dribbled by the offensive team. I will detail later in the diagram chapter. Again, I emphasize if you have previously taught solid man-to-man principles, your zones will be that much more proficient.

The zone defense that is probably used the most is the 2-1-2 or 2-3 alignment. Other alignments include the 1-3-1, the 1-2-2, and the 3-2. What determines which alignment to play? The answer is multitudinous but includes the talent of your players as well as the opponents, the offensive alignment of the foe, and their strengths.

Adjust your zone to meet the alignment and strengths. That is the advantage of being able to play multiple zone defenses. However, if your team is limited in talent, keep it simple and play what your team does best.

To better teach various zone defensive alignments, I found it is very advisable to divide the court lengthwise into three sections. They are the middle lane as defined by the width of the foul lane. Then the two outside lanes as defined by the outside boundary line and the foul lane line on each side. This definitively makes it easier to assign individual responsibilities in each different zone defense alignment. There are "rules" for each defender in each location in the defense and they are dependent on the location of the ball. One general rule is, unless otherwise directed, each individual defender will pressure the ball in an aggressive man-to-man fashion when the ball is in their area. Another general rule is, EVERY TIME THE BALL CHANGES POSITION BY PASS OR DRIBBLE, ALL FIVE DEFENSIVE PLAYERS MUST ALTER THEIR POSITION ACCORDINGLY TO DEFEND. To repeat, ALL FIVE, EVERY TIME! Let me warn you at this juncture that often zone defenders tend to become lax and less aggressive in a zone than while playing pressure man-to-man. Do not let this occur. NEVER LET THEM REST OR LOAF ON DEFENSE REGARDLESS OF THE ASSIGNMENT!

There are specific rules for each defender in each defensive alignment. They are spelled out in the various diagrams to follow.

Again, they are determined by the position of the ball and the position of the defender in the defense. Instruct your players in these rules. I have attempted to keep them as simple as possible.

Here is a valuable teaching technique to aid your instruction of the players as they attempt to learn the various slides of each zone formation. The coach should stand out-of-bounds under the basket being defended and face inward toward the court. Have five defenders form whatever defensive alignment you want to teach, i.e., 2-1-2, 2-3, 1-3-1, 1-2-2, or 3-2. There are seven general areas where the offensive team will locate the ball by passing or dribbling. They are right and left corner, right and left wing, point or front, high post, and low post. With these locations in mind, the coach, while under the basket, yells out the various locations of the ball, such as "right wing," "point," "left corner" etc. The coach observes how the five defenders move after each command. In the beginning, give the commands slowly and correct mistakes. As the players begin to better comprehend the slides, increase the tempo and again, correct as needed. You can also have an assistant coach or a player with a ball located at points of attack of the zone. After you give several commands, shout, "SHOT," and have the person with the ball shoot at the basket. All five defenders then position themselves to rebound. Later, you can even have them rebound and fast break to the other basket. Bring on another five players and repeat.

Once again, I caution not to teach beyond the level of the abilities and understandings of your team. If you choose to teach multiple defenses, it is not the total number of defenses you attempt to play. IT IS THE NUMBER OF DEFENSES YOUR TEAM PLAYS WELL! I have mentioned four different zone alignments plus man-to-man. Remember it takes time and patience to teach defense. If you also choose to add various presses to your defensive repertoire, it will more than fill your defensive basket. Therefore, select wisely as to the number of defenses you wish to use effectively. A limited number of defenses your team can play correctly is much better than many defenses played haphazardly.

BE WELL COACHED DEFENSIVELY! This result will be because you, as coach, did your job daily. You saw to it that your players learned what you taught and were able to put that knowledge to good use. Review the laws of learning in Chapter 3.

Here are three of the more important goals of the zone defense.

First, do not allow the offense to beat the defense back to the scoring area with numbers, that is, more offensive players than defensive. Ideally, you want to have all five defenders in place. Of course, that will not always happen. Thus, practice the 2-on-1 and 3-on-2 drills often. Another method is to emphasize defensive transition, whereby all five defenders must retreat to a point below the foul line when you blow your whistle during any offensive drill. Have them place the ball on the floor regardless and SPRINT!

Second, teach defensive blocking out and rebounding. It is not practical to play excellent defense and then allow "put backs" by the offensive team for easy scores. I believe it is vital for all five defenders to rebound unless you have a large height advantage over the opponents. This is a choice.

Third, when your team is playing against a zone, you should teach getting the ball inside the perimeter of the defense by either pass or dribble. Therefore, on defense you must teach the reverse by preventing penetration. Especially prevent the pass to the post player. Read these fundamentals again in Chapter 9. In order to stop dribble penetration, here are some helpful hints:

    A. Do not let your perimeter players "gamble" by reaching to constantly attempt to steal the ball. Yes, pressure the dribbler or passer, but play solid man-to-man on the ball. Keep the player with the ball in front of the defender.

B. If the defensive slide is an extra-long one, do not "run" at the offensive player. Use proper footwork (see advance step, Chapter 7), so the defender can quickly change direction in case of a dribble.

Over the years as I have observed various zone defense teams, I became mindful of a big weakness by many. What? They allowed the foul lane defender to merely stay in the lane and guard an exceedingly small area. I strongly believe that defender needs to have more responsibility. To be more efficiently contributory to the total team defense, they must guard a "triangular" area. This area ranges from outside the low block on one side of the lane, to the center of the foul line, to the block on the other of the basket. Review "Post Defense" in Chapter 9. I used to say, "Guard more than a dime's worth." That is exactly what transpires by simply standing in the lane in front of the basket. Teach this player to be much more alert and aggressive, and most importantly, what to do to accomplish. Very often the defender should be practically playing man-to-man if the offense positions a talented player in the post area. See Chapter 9. Lastly, this player must be a primary defensive rebounder.

As much as possible, attempt to match up with the alignment of the offensive players. Unless trapping, there should never be two defenders guarding the ball. This does happen often when you are playing an even numbered front alignment, like the 2-3 zone. Be positive that your two front defenders know who is to guard the one offensive player in their area with the ball.

It is prime to know the best perimeter shooters on the offense team, so as to "favor" their area. Sometimes you must have your defenders "cheat" on their slides away from these players in order to better shut down these scorers. Choose to have someone else beat you or take the most shots in that undertaking.

It is fairly easy to play a situational trap defense from a zone alignment. We used to spring a trap against some teams every time the ball was passed to an offensive player in either baseline corner of the scoring area. I numbered my defenses. Therefore, I just added a "T" after the number to indicate using our trapping defense from that zone. For example, our #2 defense was 2-3 or 2-1-2 zone. If we said, "2T," this meant we were automatically going to trap whenever the offense passed the ball into the baseline corner area. Also, as I described in Chapter 9, when the ball was successfully passed into the post area, we could choose to double team (trap) the post player if we were getting hurt by the player. See diagram chapter for proper slides of our "T" defenses.

Again, I emphasize that you must get every player in your zone defenses to hustle. I would always try to induce that extra reserved exertion whenever we played zone. I would often exhort our zone defenders, "Make them think we have six defenders on the court due to our aggressive, alert play." It is wonderful to witness when it occurs. MAKE IT HAPPEN! Always play the players who demonstrate to you this exceptional, conscious effort.

To summarize this chapter, let me conclude, that although I strongly urge you to teach man-to-man defensive basics first, zone defense is often effective to gain victories. After every game we played, I would write a synopsis in a notebook. I would state what defenses and offenses the opponents used, and the same for my team, along with other pertinent comments. Commonly, the reason we won many games was, "Our zone defenses." However, I persistently credit that it was because we were an excellent man-to-man defensive team first. Therefore, do not shy away from teaching some zone, but do not skip the first step. I hope some of this advice is helpful in strengthening your zone endeavors.

CHAPTER 12

GENERAL OFFENSIVE FUNDAMENTALS AND TECHNIQUES

I have purposefully decided in advance not to include a host of offensive formation, patterns or plays to use versus a variety of defenses in this book. The reasoning is simple: there are just too many. Therefore, read, research, investigate, and inquire of others or merely use your own imaginative thoughts and ideas to accomplish this goal. However, I will suggest some "dos and don'ts." Thus, here are some helpful hints to teach against any scoring area defense.

1. Use the dribble as a weapon to advance the ball toward the basket or to obtain a better passing angle. Eliminate the "one bounce habit" or the dribble in place for the sake of

merely bouncing the ball. This accomplishes nothing!

2. Advance the ball close to the defense in order to more easily pass by a defender. Inexperienced players shy away from this skill. Enforce this.

3. Teach all dribblers court vision. That is head up and eyes front in order to see all in front of them. This enables them to make better choices with the ball. During dribbling drills, be sure to emphasis this skill. No looking at the ball. Practice using both the right and left hand. Protect the ball.

4. Teach all the "triple threat" positions with the ball. This is a must for any player who possesses the ball, but has not dribbled. The offensive player stands with knees flexed, feet shoulder width apart, both hands on the ball about chin level, and facing the defense. From this position, the offensive player is a threat to the defense to shoot, dribble or pass to a teammate.

5. Teach all, but especially your guards, how to handle the double team.

6. Setting screens, or "picks" is an established principle for a successful offence. You must teach players how to screen and not take it

for granted. By definition, a screen is to LEGALLY establish a stationary position BETWEEN a defender and another teammate in order to impede the movement of the defender. This is done to give the teammate an open shot, or a cut to the ball to receive a pass. Inexperienced players often screen their teammate instead of the teammate's defender. Teach what is necessary, who to screen and how. It is prudent for you, the coach, to read the rule book concerning screens. An illegal screen will cost your team possession of the ball, a team foul and a personal foul on the offending player.

7. While we are discussing screens, players must be taught how to use screens. To properly do so, the cutter using the screen must cut as close to the screener as possible to prevent his or her defender from getting through the screen. Do not allow the cutter to "LOOP" around the screen. Another common mistake is not waiting for the screen to get to the recipient. That player must wait until the screen is set and then cut sharply over it for it to achieve its purpose.

8. Teach proper shooting form for jump shots, free throws and especially layups. See chapter on shooting for more details. The layup shot is taken for granted because the

shooter is so close to the basket. Young players will have trouble shooting with the "off" hand, right handers with the left and left with the right. A good rule to follow and teach is opposite foot-opposite hand. To shoot a right-hand layup, take off on the left foot and shoot with the right hand. Conversely, to shoot a left-hand layup, take off on the right foot. For players experiencing difficulty, here is an easy drill to help. Have the player stand with their feet together and ball in hand on either side of the basket. To teach right hand, player steps with left foot, rises with the ball in both hands, and releases with the right hand. On the left side of the basket, player steps with right foot, rise and then release with the left hand. The next progression is to have the player move back a little from the basket, take one dribble, and then repeat the actions explained above. Hopefully with this progression, the player will acquire the footwork timing necessary to shoot the shot under game speed conditions.

9. Another teaching point concerning layups is to make sure shooters take the ball up with both hands as high as possible and aim the released ball into the square above the Goal on the backboard, softly and high. Insist on proper form in practice. Layups are "money

in the bank," and best of all, points on the scoreboard!

10. Another shot that players neglect to practice enough is the free throw. Like all shots, there are some basic fundamentals to follow. Here are some: as little ball movement as possible; shooting forearm forms a right angle at the elbow with the upper arm; shoot the ball with a soft, high arc to clear the front rim of the basket; ball should be released by the middle and forefinger of the shooting hand; head over the feet and lean into the shot upon release. I use to tell my players, "If you are making an acceptable percentage, I really am not concerned with fundamentals." However, I would insist to those not shooting well, "You have got to change your methods to improve."

11. Teach players to shoot within their individual range. Not everyone is a 3-point shooter, though most all think they are. Bad shots always hurt teams. Most of the time, the results are a turnover.

12. Teach the V and L cut footwork (see Chapter 4).

13. Teach and emphasize all rules pertaining to offense, as most result in loss of ball if violated Here is a list:
    a. 3 second rule.
    b. 10 second rule.
    c. Backcourt rule.
    d. 5 second throw-in rule.
    e. Spot throw-in rule.
    f. Rules pertaining to the foul lane during a free throw.
    g. Palming the ball during dribbling.
    h. Closely guarded player while dribbling or holding the ball.
    i. Fumble, dribble, fumble, recover the ball - LEGAL Dribble, fumble, recover - LEGAL
        Dribble, fumble, dribble - VIOLATION.
    j. Throw-ins from the sidelines are always a spot throw-in. From baseline after a successful field goal or free throw allows the throw-in player to move off the spot.
    k. Stepping on or over the baseline, or sideline, or handing off the ball to a player in-bounds, during a throw-in - VIOLATION.
    l. Excessive swinging of the elbows while in possession of the ball - VIOLATION.
    m. Proper and improper screening - VIOLATION

14. If possible, have a certified referee hold a rules clinic for your team prior to the opening of the season.

In summary of this chapter, I say, "LITTLE THINGS MEAN A LOT!" A little occurrence, omission, or mistake in a crucial spot in a crucial game, could be the difference in a WIN or DEFEAT. To sum it up in different words, "AN OUNCE OF PREVENTION IS WORTH A POUND OF CURE!" Therefore, prepare your team. There is more to coaching basketball than running, dribbling, jumping, shooting, and passing! Make a check list of items to cover preseason and use it. As is the Boy Scouts' motto, "BE PREPARED!" This is certainly sage advice for basketball players and coaches.

CHAPTER 13

ATTACKING MAN-TO-MAN DEFENSES

The object of a basketball game is for one team to score more points than their opponents. Therefore, you must teach and drill your players in basketball offensive fundamentals. These essentials to include dribbling, passing, catching, and shooting. Encompass drills to improve these skills every day in your practice schedule, especially if your squad is young and inexperienced. Your team cannot score if its members have difficulty dribbling, passing, and catching the ball under pressure. Design drills that emphasize practicing like your team must play. Such as one-on-one dribbling drills, passing past a defender to a receiving teammate, relieving pressure from a defender by using a V-cut, and a variety of other shooting lessons.

One excellent way to accomplish this amount of work in the shortest amount of time is the STATION method. If you are fortunate enough to have multiple basket areas in your practice facility, designate a daily drill at each area with a five- or six-minute allotted time limit period and the particular skill fundamental you wish practiced. Assign a small group at each area, time carefully, and blow the whistle to signal the players to rotate to next station. Thus, in 20 to 24 minutes, you complete four different offensive drills. You can do this with defensive drills as well. If you are favored with assistant coaches or volunteers, assign them to a station after you have indoctrinated them thoroughly as to what to emphasize in the various drills. Otherwise, you monitor the stations as closely as possible and make corrections as you do. Do not allow bad habits to be practiced. Be sure to explain each drill with proper terminology and give each drill a name.

It is a given that preseason practices in most public high schools, or even middle schools, are usually short. They are three to four weeks at best prior to the first regular season game. Therefore, in planning your practice schedule, especially for an inexperienced group, go slowly, but efficiently. Your preseason practices are especially important. In fact, they are probably the most meaningful segment of the season. Why? Because your team should be forming routines and habits which they will be executing the entire season. Consequently, make all habits good ones. To do this, you must sometimes have a "drill sergeant" mentality to accomplish lasting positive results. I urge you to go back to Chapter 1 and re-read the advice I wrote on the adoption of a coaching philosophy. Some of the points I mentioned there may be helpful in this area.

As I stated in an earlier chapter, "Attacking Zone Defenses," there are a host of alignments to utilize versus a man-to-man defense. Thus, I make no effort to diagram any here. I will offer some of the simpler ones.

1. 3 out-2 in. With three-man weave. Usually, this is a three guard or better ball handlers' offense. The idea is to keep the middle of the offensive area open for a dribble penetration.

2. Post. If you have a taller player, or any player, who can play with their back to the basket, operate your offense around that player receiving the ball as often as possible, either to shoot or pass.

3. Pass and Screen Away or Pass and Screen on the Ball. This is a simple offense. The title tells the story. The passer screens the nearest player away from the pass receiver or screens the defender guarding the receiver of the pass.

4. Isolation. Used when you have one or two good one-on-one players. Design situation whereby these players get one-on-one opportunities to beat their defender for a high percentage shot.

5. Spread. Similar to the 3 out-2 in alignment. Instead of a three-person weave, when a player passes to another, that player cuts hard to the basket. Players stay spread out as best as possible with good spacing. When a player does cut, another player fills that spot to maintain floor balance.

6. Designated Plays. Give a name, a number, or letter to certain actions for certain players. For example, X, UP, DOUBLE, 22(a player's number), red, etc. The main problem with this scenario is if the play does not work, the offense is left with no options and must reset or freelance. However, without getting too detailed, options can be part of the scheme. Use your judgment.

To prevent #6 from occurring, teams often adopt what is called "pattern" or "continuity" offenses. In this type of offense, all five players have "rules" for a certain action of a pass or location of the ball. The "pattern" flows as the players pass, screen, and cut until a good shot is obtained. I was a very strong advocate of this type of offense and used three or four different ones over the years with success. I found that the players greatly enjoyed this method. Note: you can also use #6 above within the pattern, if desired or needed. Make the pattern as simple, or as intricate, as the talent and experience of your players. You be the judge of that.

Here are some of the benefits of the patterned offense as professed by Garland Pin holster in his book. "Wheel Offense for Basketball." I found these advantages in a patterned offense.

1. Offer a method of getting a high percentage shot on most possessions. No matter how good you believe your shooters are, taking "bad" shots is almost simultaneous to a turnover. All players will take these types of shots if you allow them. Also, coach your squad that sometimes, depending on "time and situation," even some open shots are "bad" shots.

2. Aids offensive rebounding. After some extensive practice, your players will anticipate what type of shot will be taken often within the pattern and beat the defense to the inside rebounding position.
3. All five players get to share the ball, pass it, and shoot it. Basketball is a TEAM sport and when each player knows that they will be involved in the offense, they get that TEAM spirit. Often a shooter gets a smile on their face when they pass for a scoring assist.

4. All players should learn how to face the basket. Your job as a coach is to train your players to become as proficient with this skill as possible. The pattern offense promotes

player movement without the ball. This is especially good for your so called "big people." These types of players cannot develop if they are allowed to plant themselves in a confined area and just operate in limited space. They must be taught to be "athletic."

5. This type of offense forces all five defensive players to actual play defense. With all five of your players moving and cutting at some moment in your offense, the defenders, must adjust to this. Very often, one of your inside players will get an inside defender in a position that they are not used to defending. The same is true for a defending guard having to defend in the post position. I used to call time outs often when my team would "bog down" and tell them simply, "MAKE THEM PLAY DEFENSE!" That meant make the extra pass, the extra cut until we forced a defensive mistake. If your team is patient, that mistake will occur.

6. Speed can easily be used to control the tempo of the game. I have always declared to my teams, "We have to be able to play fast at times, and to play slow if necessary." We merely executed our pattern by moving, cutting, and passing for more extended time when we wanted to play slow. In my junior

college coaching days, we had to play Allegheny from Pittsburgh for the Region 20 Juco championship. They were 24-0 year to date when we played them. This game was in 1982 before the shot clock was used. With about seven minutes remaining in the first half and Allegheny leading us by a slim margin, I called time out. I told my players, "Run our White offense and take the last shot!" Yes, hold the ball for seven long minutes!

My reasoning was that his team on paper was better than we were, and I was very satisfied at this juncture of the game to be as close as we were. My team did as they were directed and performed perfectly. Moving on to near end of the game, we remained "in the game" against a superior opponent. With two seconds left, with the score tied, we had possession of the ball out-of-bounds at the baseline farthest from our basket. I called time out and my point guard said to me, "I want the ball." I replied, "You got it." I explained a play which had the guards aligned in tandem even with the ball. The guards cut with the point guard cutting toward the ball and circling up court along the right sidelines. Meanwhile, one of my wingmen was stationed at midcourt. After the guards cut, he broke hard toward the ball and the passer out-of-bounds threw the ball to him. After catching, he touched passed to his left to the point guard racing up the sideline. The guard caught the ball near midcourt, shot immediately, and yes, the ball went in our basket for the win!

We would not be able to "possess" the ball without shooting today because of the shot clock in college circles. In boys' high school and recreational ball, there is no shot clock, so you do have that option. Maybe not the extremes that I did, but to some extent. Teach your teams to play slow. You never know when that will be necessary to win a game.

I would like to mention at this point that when I felt we had the best team and a team attempted to slow us down by "holding the ball" in order to shorten the game, I did not allow them. I would press them full court at every opportunity. Do not let a team dictate game tempo to you. Refer to Chapter 5 concerning my defensive philosophy. There I state that our defense must be able to take charge of the opponents' offense. Since we were a winning team most seasons, we often had to employ this strategy.

7. Presents Options Within the Pattern to Score. You can insert some individual "plays" in the pattern structure for what I would call "quick hitters." These are good to use at the

beginning of games, quarters, after time outs, when there is little time on the clock, and for a last shot before time expires.

8. Forces Opponents to Switch on Defense. If your team can run your pattern well, with good timing and excellent use of screens, the opponent often has to switch defensive assignments. This often presents mismatches for your team to take advantage of.

9. Promotes Teamwork and Spirit. In pattern play, the players soon grasp the team feeling of sharing the ball with good passing and cutting to receiving the ball. As they cut, they know that they will get the ball, so they cut and play aggressively to be successful.

10. Easy to Practice - Dry Run It Daily.

11. Teach the Whole, Then Break Down the Parts in Drill Form. You will discover that no matter how simple your offense attacks are, your players will have difficulty implementing them under game pressure conditions. This is even truer when your opponents are a very proficient pressure man-to-man defensive team. It is amazingly easy to diagram plays, but the pencil, pen or chalk do not play, people do. Your guards, who do most of the ball handling to advance

the ball up court, must be taught how to handle pressure defenses. This is a MUST in order to get the players and the ball in the proper area to initiate the offense. Otherwise, the defense is dictating to your team. Then your team and your offensive plays or patterns are disrupted, and chaos ensues. Therefore, once your choice of attack is determined and taught as a whole, without pressure, from that point onward, NEVER practice your offense without pressure defense. This prepares your team properly and gives them the confidence needed when pressure is applied by their opponents. This always happens when they are behind in the closing moments of the game. Teach procedure first and then offensive attack, no matter what it is. Do not skip this step.

The most demanding feat, particularly for less skilled players, is getting the ball in the proper area of the court in order to "get into the offense." Even with this accomplished, you will discover very quickly that your team will be negligent in "running the offense" to your satisfaction. This is primarily caused by impatience, lack of skill, insufficient practice, good defense, and poor acceptance of the attack by a player or two. You, as coach, must figure out why and adjust as needed. Have forbearance in and confidence with your philosophy of attack and drill, drill, drill!

In the diagram chapter, I have given you an easy and proven way for your guards to advance the ball up court against pressure defense. Thus, allowing them to get the ball in the proper area of the front court to initiate the offense. This is a must, so practice it, and practice it often. Briefly, once a guard in bounds has the ball, they should pause to allow the other guard and all others to clear to the front area of the guard with the ball. Then they have room to dribble to the wide side of the back court and advance up court. The guard who cleared out must watch to see if their partner can easily accomplish this. If not, they should cut back and hook to receive a pass. Then allow the passer to clear in front of them and dribble up court using the wide side. If the defense is extra tough, the partner guards may have to repeat as needed. Remember, they have 10 seconds to get past the midcourt line. I named this action, "Blue" as an alert to the players. Use any term you desire.

CHAPTER 14

ATTACKING ZONE DEFENSES

To beat various zone defenses; you must do at least some or all these offensive techniques. They are:

1. Advance the ball forward enough to make ALL FIVE offensive players a threat to score. Very often, particularly with inexperienced players, the ball handling front perimeter personnel become just that, ball handlers and passers.

2. Keep the ball moving if not a threat to dribble drive or shoot.

3. Overload a scoring area. Put more offensive players in a triangular formation than defenders in the area.

4. Move, or cut, offensive players from one area to another as the ball is being passed around the perimeter of the defense.

5. All zones have gaps, or holes, which is space between two defenders. Place your players in these gaps or cut to gaps.

6. If an offensive player is in a gap and is not going to cut after passing the ball, they must step forward closer to the basket. This is done so that player is more of a threat to shoot, and hopefully score once the ball is received back.

7. It is a must that all perimeter players always assume a triple threat position while in possession of the ball. This makes them a threat to shoot, pass, or dribble.

8. You hurt zones by getting the ball past the perimeter of the defense. This is done either with a dribble drive or pass. On the dribble drive, the player often only has to beat one defender to obtain a short jump shot. Most time the dribbler will not get to the basket for a layup, but will get a high percentage shot, or will be able to pass to an open teammate.

9. If your offensive alignment calls for a middle post player, then passing the ball to this

player is another excellent way of getting the ball into the middle of the zone.

Here is more detailed information concerning #9. Have this player stay low opposite the ball and then flash cut to an open area once the zone shifts on the perimeter ball movement. The zone defenders almost always have their backs to the post player as they follow the ball movement. Therefore, instruct the post to be patient before they flash cut. Remember, the offense is often designed to get the ball to the post as often as possible. Therefore, the post must get open often to receive the ball. If the post moves in a circular fashion as the ball is being passed in a similar manner around the perimeter of the defense, it becomes more difficult for the post to be open. If the post flash cuts and does not receive a pass, repeat the process described above.

Here is another useful suggestion for the post when they receive a pass and are defended well. The post should look opposite to pass. In other words, when receiving from the left, look right wing area. If receiving from the right, look left wing area. Usually there is an open teammate in one of the two spots. Other advice is to not hold the ball or dribble in congestion. Whenever the post receives the ball, they will instantly attract much defensive attention. To counteract, make quick decisions, i.e., quick pass, quick shot, or quick move to the basket.

Due to the very nature of zone defenses, all five defenders are usually "packed in" a limited space, the scoring area. This restricts your team's ability to obtain a high percentage shot. It also causes your players to be patient, make more passes, and confine dribbling. Yes, a much lower percentage shot is always available from a longer distance from the basket after one pass. In truth, that is one of the objectives of the zone. To force the offense to take long range shots over the zone. What is the answer to the defense's strategy? Two words - PATIENCE & EXECUTION!

Early on in this chapter, I listed some offensive procedures as aids to beat the zone. Incorporate some of these into an offensive pattern or two and attack the zone. Your team must be taught in advance that most likely it will take several passes and some strategic maneuvering of players to obtain the shots your team desires. MAKE THE DEFENSE PLAY DEFENSE! If your team is patient, usually one of the five defenders will make a mistake and your team capitalizes. Do not just talk the strategy, practice it. Players are never hesitant to shoot. Make sure your team is taking shots they can make. This is especially true if your team is a poor offensive rebounding team or lacks outside shooting abilities.

I have decided in advance not to include very many offensive diagrams in this book. I did so because of the inordinate number of alignments, and in turn, plans of attack that are possibilities to include in a team's arsenal. My advice is to keep it as simple as possible, especially for the inexperienced players. I have presented some uncomplicated, but effective recommendations that can serve as a start for your team. Here are a few that can be used against zones.

Initially, invoke a "rule" that has your team use one guard versus an even person zone front or two guards against an odd numbered front. For instance, use one guard when facing a 2-1-2 or 2-3 and two guards versus a 1-2-2, 1-3-1 or 3-2. Generally, you would want more offensive players where the zone has fewer defenders. Using this "rule" will allow you to do this. You can accomplish the overload effect two ways. They are placing the offensive players and merely keep moving the ball. A better method is moving or cutting players to areas to cause an overload as well as moving the ball - move people and the ball.

The most commonly used alignment against the even numbered front zone is the 1-3-1. Following the two-guard front "rule," there are two clever ways to obtain the overload effect you desire. You can begin with two guards out front, thus giving you a 2-3 setup versus a 2-1-2 or a 2-3 zone. After a guard passes to a wing on the same side of the defense, they cut to the baseline on that same side. The other guard moves to or near the elbow area of the ball side. This gives you the overload on that side of the defense, in effect, the desired 1-3-1. If the ball is returned to the guard near the elbow area. They should reverse the ball to the other side of the defense by dribbling toward the other elbow area and pass to the wing on that side of the defense. The guard merely follows their pass and cuts through to the baseline. That triggers the other guard to cut from the opposite baseline to the elbow area on the ball side. Now you have accomplished the same 1-3-1 alignment.

Earlier in this chapter, I described how your post player should operate versus a zone. Review this explanation and coach your post accordingly. This will make your 1-3-1 overload more effective, especially if your team is able to get the ball to the post for a shot or a pass opposite from the post.

Another simple way to transfer the overload from one side of the defense to the other, is to place the 1-3-1 versus the zone. Then, have the baseline player be a "rover" from one side of the defense to the other. In other words, as the ball is passed from the overloaded side to the front guard and reversed to the opposite side of the defense, the baseline player cuts along the baseline to the ball side. If you use this method, place your best shooter as the "rover." If your guards are the better shooters, use the cutting guard to the baseline method. That guard can then become the "rover." This latter method affords you a little more variety in your offense against even numbered fronts.

Here is another easy offensive alignment to teach that can be used against an odd numbered front such as the 1-3-1, 1-2-2 or 3-2 zone. I called this "3-low." Place the two-guard offensive players in the gaps of the odd person front. Now place your three remaining players in the "3-low" formation along the baseline where there is only one or two defenders. This automatically gives you an overload on the baseline area. To further gain an advantage, screen the one defender as in the 1-3-1, or the two defenders as in the

3-2 or 1-2-2 zones. Do this screening as the ball is passed from one front guard to the other. When this pass is made, the on-side baseline player screens a defender closest to them and the center baseliner does a "fish-hook" cut around the screener to receive a pass from a guard for a shot or a short dump in pass to the screener. Teach the guards not to pass back and forth quickly, but to wait for the screen and cut on the baseline. If the defenders stop it, just pass to the other guard, and repeat the baseline screen and cut on the other side.

Another variation is to place two offensive players on each side of the foul lane on the blocks and then have the third be a rover. The rover receives screens from the players on the blocks as the ball is moved from guard to guard. If the defenders attempt to defend the rover, this will leave the player on the block to receive a direct pass from a guard, or from the rover after they receive a pass and are defended. Rather simple, but it works with patience.

In summation of this chapter, I discovered during my coaching career that far more opponents relied on zone defenses than man-to-man. As I have related elsewhere in this book, teaching effective man-to-man defense is time consuming and hard work. Thus, many coaches take the easier route of zone defense. There are some other reasons as well. It is easier to "hide" a less skilled defense player in a zone. In addition, most likely teams playing zone will commit less person fouls. Some would also argue that it is more efficient to rebound defensively from a zone since all five defenders are close to the scoring area. Another plus is some teams fast break well from a zone. Of course, there are pluses and minuses in all defenses. Since these are reasons to play zones, prepare your team wisely to play against them because you are sure to have to face them.

CHAPTER 15

HOW TO BEAT THE FULL COURT ZONE PRESS DEFENSE

As a preface for this chapter, why do teams press using full court zone defenses? There could be multiple reasons. Here are some:
1. When a team is behind. This may happen at any juncture of the game, but usually in last few minutes.
2. To up tempo the game.
3. To surprise a team.
4. To begin the second half.
5. After special situations like a successful foul shot, field goal or a time out.
6. To cause a team to discontinue their regular offense.
7. A few teams may use a special press group.

8. The zone press could be a team's major defense.
9. The opponents are less talented than the pressing team.

I included this chapter because it is very discouraging for a team to work diligently to get ahead of the opponent, then to have a zone press thrown at them and lose the game. Why? It is because of poor preparation to face and handle the defense. To prevent this kind of defeat, you must have a plan and prepare in detail.

I warn you; it is difficult to practice a press offense. What do I mean? Your "second" team or substitutes are most likely not as talented as your opponents' starting five. Plus, the defenses you must set up to practice against are by no means as skilled as the defenses your team is going to face in games. It is plain common sense. Therefore, all the more reason your team must be very disciplined, knowledgeable, and apt to be successful versus the full court zone presses. I did my utmost to design an offense that was simple, had options, and was capable of countering what the defenses were attempting to do. Of course, we had to execute.

I would tell my team that beating a full court zone press can be contrasted with an NFL quarterback. For the football quarterback to be successful in completing passes, he must know where his potential receivers are located. Hence, these receivers run designated passing routes and the quarterback knows where in advance.

In basketball, each player with the ball against the press has a better chance of success if they know in advance where the potential receivers are positioned. Over the years, I have watched teams get demolished versus the zone press due to a helter-skelter, "run to the four winds" type of attack. Additionally, there was usually a lot of needless head down dribbling into trouble as well as some soft or lob passes. As I have stated, one of the reasons to press is to up tempo the game and cause the offense to disband their normal routine.

So, what do you do? My answer is to have an offensive pattern whereby each player with the ball knows in advance where their potential receivers are situated on the court. Plus, the receivers know where to go and the passers are aware of what to do after completing a pass. Before I proceed with this explanation, let us discuss the passers and receivers. I will begin with the passers.

    A. The player with the ball out-of-bounds has five seconds to complete a pass to a teammate in bounds. Five seconds is not as short of a period as many think. Suggestion: Gather all your players around you and tell them to shut their eyes. On your signal, start counting to five and instruct them to raise their hands when each feel that five seconds have expired. You will be surprised at the results. Do the same with 10 seconds, the amount of time your team has to get the ball across the midcourt line into frontcourt. Again, the results will be varied. Remind your team each second is counted as "one thousand one, one thousand two, etc.," not a quick "1, 2, 3, 4, 5." Stress with your team that rushing and panic is not necessary or tolerated. Be forceful in explaining to your squad that it is much better for them to receive a five or ten second violation call against them than to hurry and make an errant pass to a defender that could result in a quick score. That way the other team has to take the ball out-of-bounds and we can set our defense. Best of all, the score on the score board does not change. Remember that this passer can move sideways out-of-bounds along the baseline after a successful foul shot or field goal by the opponents. This potential maneuver is often a big aid in successfully bounding the ball within the time limit. Make sure it is included and practiced in your zone press offense. There are four potential receivers in bounds. Practice making good passes to each of them.

B. Once the ball is in bounded to one of the four, that receiver must expect a quick double team or trap. What I am going to say next may be the most important point concerning beating the zone press. THE FIRST THING THE RECEIVER MUST DO IS CATCH THE BALL AND PIVOT TO FACE

UP COURT! This will allow that receiver to see the full court ahead and other possible receivers. All too often, the first thing this receiver does is to take off dribbling, usually with their head down and out of control. I will admit that if your team possesses an exceptional dribbler, note I said exceptional, then sometimes when that player is the receiver, they may choose to beat the press by dribbling through it. Make that option selectively.

You must practice passing from out of a double team because once the ball is in bounded, it is game on to beat the press. See the explanation of the "Close the Gate" drill in the NOTE of the "Bulls in the Ring" drill, Chapter 17.

Form groups of four within your squad. One player has a ball, two players stand beside a receiver about eight to ten feet away. The player with the ball passes to the receiver. As soon as the receiver catches the pass, the two standbys "close the gate" and double team the receiver aggressively. The player being trapped must keep on balance; ball tucked under their chin with elbows away from the body. That player must be STRONG with the ball. Do not allow the ball to be away from the body and stay there, especially overhead. If and when the ball goes there, the player does so to pass quickly. In traps, defensive players are taught to trace the position of the ball with hands and arms close together. Their objective is to tip and deflect the pass. Wherever the ball is located in the passer's hands, that is most likely where the defenders' hands and arms will be. Therefore, instruct the passers to keep the ball in close, elbows and arms moving with a strong grip on the ball. Sometimes it is possible to step through the two defenders and split the double team to complete a pass. Once a pass is successfully completed out of the double team back to the original passer, the two trappers now run to this player and double team. Continue and then switch trappers to passers and receivers to trappers, until all have adequate practice. Hint: NO LOB PASSES ALLOWED.

The zone press defense is a gamble defense if it does involve double teams. Five defenders must defend the entire length of the court, 84 feet for high school and 92 feet college. Usually, the objective is to get a quick interception. If the press is not successful after two or three passes in the back court, most likely your team has "broken" the press. In my zone press offense, once the ball arrives at the center court area, we would attack with a dribble and a 3 on 1 (or 2), and hopefully a successful shot.

See the diagram chapter as to the starting alignment of the four potential receivers in bounds with the ball out-of-bounds at the baseline. The two guards line up facing their teammate, who is in bounding the ball, at the junctures of the foul line and the foul lane. The other two players position themselves just below the center circle and face the ball. They have a choice. Line up one player beside the other, or one player in front of the other. When the out-of-bounds player slaps the ball, the guard closest to the ball sets a back screen for the other guard, who MUST wait until the screen is set. This guard screens, then, and not before, the other guard cuts off the screen to a receiving area. That area should be between the lower half of the foul lane and the corner. DO NOT CUT TO THE CORNER! That is where the defense would prefer the player to receive the ball. The double team becomes more dangerous here. After the first guard has cut, the screening guard steps directly toward the ball to receive a short bounce pass if the first cutter is not open. There is a tendency for these two guards to rush and move simultaneously. Practice diligently and make these two be patient with their movements. After both guards have carried out their duties, the inbounds passer has two options.

After the guards have moved, and not before, the other two at midcourt move. One cuts towards the middle of the outside lane on the ball side and the other cuts to the opposite outside lane. Now you have four potential receivers. At this point, I numbered those receivers for practice and drill purposes. #1 would be the guard who used the guard screen and cut toward the ball. #2 would be the guard who set the screen for #1. #3 would be the player closest to #1 in the outside lane. #4 would be the player farthest from the ball when out-of-bounds. Of course, #5 is the player taking the ball out-of-bounds.

What I have described so far surmises the defense faced is a 1-2-2 or a 1-2-1-1 alignment, with a defender in front of #5 and #1, and #2 closely guarded. That is why you will need a screen to free one of them. If the defense allows an uncontested throw in by #5, then #1 or #2 will get the pass and the other immediately cuts to the middle area. This offense ALWAYS has a guard in the middle. The middle of the defense is where any zone defense is liable to detrimental consequences if a pass penetrates there. Most times, your guards are your best ball handlers. You will see as the ball progresses down court; it is greatly beneficial to have a good ball handler in the middle of the defense.

Now, let us attack this full court zone press defense. I will take the on court receivers in numerical order. If #1 gets the first pass, #2 immediately cuts to the middle. #1 catches, pivots, and faces up court to see his possible receivers, #3 and #2, both 10 to 12 feet away in triangular fashion. #5 always does the same thing regardless of who has the ball. They become the trailer or the safety valve when the ball needs to be reversed if the nearest receivers are covered. #5 should be below the line of the ball, (see definition in Chapter 4), and close enough to receive a reverse pass. #5 is almost always open.

If #2 had received the first pass, then #1 would cut to the middle, again forming a triangle with #4. #5 again moves in bounds as the trailer. If either #1 or #2 can pass forward, they follow the pass and cut up court to an area ahead of the ball.

Suppose #1 passed to #3, #1 would cut past #3 to an open area ahead of #3. If #2 passed to #4, #2 would cut past #4 to an open area ahead of #4. Both would do likewise if passed to the guard in the middle.

Whenever the ball is passed forward to either #3 or #4, the guard in the middle automatically moves farther up court to be ahead of the line of the ball to again create a triangle effect. Most times this puts the guard in the vicinity of the midcourt circle and ahead of the ball.

We continue with a successful pass to #1, then a pass from #1 to #3 and #1 cuts past #3 to the open court ahead. Here #3 should be looking to the guard in the middle, #2, and pass to them if open. If #2 does get the pass, most probable they are able to attack with a dribble toward the foul line, along with #1 and #4, in a 3 on 1 (or 2), for a high percentage shot. If #2 cannot get the pass. #1 is open often once their cut past #3 is complete.

When #1 does get the ball, this offers another option. #1 would switch jobs with #2 as #1 dribbles toward the middle of the foul line, and #2 cuts behind #1 to the outside lane and the basket. #4 would be in the other outside lane. Again, a guard in the middle and an excellent chance for a score. The same scenario is possible on the other side of the court if #2 gets the first pass. If #2 passes to #4 and cuts up court past #4 and ahead of the ball. #1 is now in the middle and stays ahead of the ball. If #4 passes to #1, #1 should be able to attack with the dribble to get a 3 on 1 (or 2) with # 3 and #2.

If the pass from #4 goes to #2 instead of #1, #2 has the option of dribbling toward the foul line and #1 cuts behind #2 to the outside lane and the basket. Again, a guard in the middle and a good opportunity for a high percentage shot.

All the above sounds easy and often is during a game. However, that is not always the case. So, let us back up to explain other options. When attacking any zone defense, you must do some or all of the following, move the ball, move people to open areas, and get the ball in the middle of the defense. Use these threats versus the full court zone press. One other additional aspect of moving the ball is reversing the ball to cause the defense to make major shifts in their alignment. How do you do that with my zone press offense?

The answer is by using reliable #5, the trailer. #5 is always below the line of the ball and behind their teammates. #5 is always open for a pass. Image them as your point guard as if you were facing a normal drop back zone defense. When facing a full court trapping zone defense, #5 main job is to be available as an open receiver. When they receive a pass, they reverse the ball to the other side of the court. When that happens, #1 and #2, the guards, must be alert. Why? Imagine #1 receives the first pass in bounds, #2 cuts to the middle. After #1 catches, pivots, and faces up court looking for #3 ahead or #2 in the middle, they see neither open. The next option is to reverse the ball to #5. Now #5 may find it necessary to take a dribble or two in the direction of #4, who should close the distance from #5 to receive #5's pass.

Here is the point that the guards must be alert. When #1 received the first pass, #2 cut to the middle. Now as the ball is reversed to #5 and then to #4, who has moved toward the baseline, #2 leaves the middle and replaces #4. #1 then cuts to middle to replace #2. If the first pass went to #2 instead of #1, and the ball was reversed to #5, #3 must cut towards #5 to receive a pass. #1 must move to replace #3 and #2 now cuts to the middle to replace #1. Again, always a guard in the middle.

The same would occur if #1 passed to #3 and cut up court past #3 and then #3 had to reverse the ball back to #5. To repeat, #4 cuts back to receive a pass from #5, #2 replaces #4. #1 replaces #2 in the middle. If #2 passes to #4 and cuts up court ahead of the ball with #1 in the middle and #4 reverses to #5, #3 cuts back toward #5 to get the reverse pass from #5. Now #1 replaces #3 and #2 cuts to the middle to replace #1. Again, a guard in the middle.

Up to this point, I have pictured what occurs if the first pass from #5 goes to either #1 or #2. Sometimes these options are not open. This is why #3 and #4 must pause to make their moves on the slap of the ball by #5. That way either player on the side of the ball can usually find an open spot, cut towards it, and receive the first pass. This is particularly true if the defense is determined that either guard is not going to receive the first pass, or the guards do not execute properly. If the first pass goes to #3, then proceed as if #1 had received it and passed to #3. Thus, #1 automatically cuts up court ahead of #3, and #2, as designed, goes to the middle ahead of #3, forming the normal triangular effect. A similar outline holds true when #4 receives the initial pass; #2 cuts up court ahead of #4 and #1 cuts to the middle ahead of #4 as well. As usual, #5 comes in bounds and trails. When analyzed, it is as if the onside guard and wing have switched places.

There is one final alternative that seems to work very satisfactorily. As stated before, #5 is permitted to move at will behind the baseline after a successful field goal of foul shot by the opponents within five seconds. #5 takes the ball out-of-bounds on the right side of the foul lane. After slapping the ball and observing all four receivers in bounds make their cuts, #5 runs to their left along the baseline. At the instant that #2 sees #5 begin to run, they sprint up court in the outside lane as if they had passed to #4. Now, when #4 sees #5 run left along the baseline, they cut toward the baseline to receive the inbound pass from #5. This option is rarely unsuccessful. #4 is now the "guard" since #2 has taken #4's place. #1 cuts to the middle, so proceed from there. To mix it up, have #5 take the ball out-of-bounds on the left side of the foul lane. #5 would then run to his right and pass to #3. #1 would sprint up court and replace #3. #2 becomes the guard in the middle. Proceed as if #3 is now the guard.

Now let me describe to you how to drill and practice this offense as a whole. Put five players on the court in the proper spots as I demonstrated in the diagram chapter and explained earlier in this chapter. You must start slowly and build. Give #5 a ball out-of-bounds and have them slap it. As coach, you should observe how the four receivers execute their movements and do what they are supposed to do. Do this a few times with the five and then bring on five more until the entire squad has performed. When you first introduce this offense, it is a good idea to include in your practice schedule the above portion of the offense until you are satisfied. Then skip and begin with the following.

As I mentioned earlier in this chapter, I numbered the potential receivers one through four. To recall, guards are 1 and 2, wings are 3 and 4, and 5 is the in bounder with the ball. Tell your five, "#1 up court and then #2 back." What does this mean? #5 will pass first to guard #1, who will pass to #3 and cut up court past #3. To return back, #5 will pass to guard #2 who will pass to #4 and cut up court past #4. Both #3 and #4 will attempt to get the ball to guard in the middle for a 3-on-2 offensive advantage. #3 passes to guard #2 in the middle, who dribbles toward the center of foul line. #1 and #4 cut toward the basket in their respective outside lanes. One will receive a pass for a layup, or a jump shot. Now #5 rebounds the ball and takes it out-of-bounds for the return trip down court. The four possible receivers assume their proper position in court. #5 slaps the ball and this time they pass to guard #2. #2 passes to #4 and cuts up court past #4. #4 passes to #1 in the middle, who dribbles toward the center of the foul line. #2 and #3 cut toward the basket in their respective outside lanes. One will receive a pass for a layup, or a jump shot. Thus, you have #1 up and #2 back.

Now bring a second group of five on court and repeat, #1 up and #2 back. This may be all you do for a few days. Next, instruct, "#3 up and #4 back."

Meaning #3 gets the first pass up and #4 is coming back. Of course, #1 must cut ahead of #3 when they receive the pass, and #2 cuts ahead when #4 receives first pass. Continue, #3 passes to #1, who passes to guard #2 in the middle, who dribbles toward the opposite foul line. #4 and #3 cut in outside lanes to receive a pass from #2 for a layup or jump shot. Coming back, first pass goes to #4 and #2 cuts ahead of #4 and #1 cuts to middle. #4 passes to #2 and cuts ahead of #2. #2 passes to #1 in the middle, who dribbles to center of foul line. #4 and #3 cut toward the basket in their respective outside lanes. One will receive a pass for a layup or jump shot. Thus, you have #3 up and #4 back. Have all your players practice this sequence.

Next you can order reverse the ball to #5. You can do this when either #1 or #2 receives the ball. You say, "1 to 5 to 4" or "2 to 5 to 3" and have players do as I have described above when this action is necessary in a game. You can also, on occasion, ask for "1 to 3 to 4" or "2 to 4 to 5 to 3," although this is not as imperative in games as the other combinations. However, some or all the blends of passes I have explained will be used in a game depending how soft, aggressive, or skilled the zone press of the opposition is. Therefore, your team may have to be more deliberate with their passes to get the ball across the center line in 10 seconds. Put into your practice schedule any combinations you feel are going to make your team successful in beating zone presses.

I realize as you read this chapter, my offense may sound complicated. Yes, it does take several pages to explain fully. However, you will find as you explain it step by step on the court and practice it daily with "dry run" numerical progressions, your players will amaze you as to how quickly they absorb it. They will actually enjoy practicing it. Of course, you eventually have to put a defense on the court for them to practice against. Once I felt that most of the players knew what to do, I would sometimes put six or seven defenders on court for the offense to beat. I found that they may not score easily, but their passing and finding an open receiver improved.

I have attempted to diagram all the options in the diagram chapter. To conclude this chapter, here are strong points of emphasis and coaching pointers in teaching this offense.

1. Make sure your guards, #1 and #2, know how to handle double teams.

2. On the slap of the ball by #5, guards go first and then #3 and #4. Not all four at once.

3. IMPORTANT! Each player who receives a pass must then pivot and face up court without dribbling, particularly the first receiver.

4. There must ALWAYS be a guard, #1 or #2, in the middle.

5. NO LOB or SOFT PASSES ALLOWED!

6. #5 is ALWAYS in the trailer or safety position.

7. As soon as #5 runs the baseline, the ball side guard cuts up court ahead of #4 or #3.

8. When a pass goes quickly to a guard, #1 or #2, in the middle at the midcourt area, attack with a dribble toward the basket with a 3 on 1 (2).

9. Remember that 10 seconds is a relatively "long" time, so do not panic or rush needlessly.

10. #5 is always open for a pass. Also, they may have to take a dribble or two to reverse the ball.

An aggressive, full court zone pressing defense is often a "gamble" defense. Thus, take advantage and attack it rather than let the defense win with mistakes by your team.

In 2015, I moved to Florida and was hired as an assistant coach at a nearby private high school. The head coach there used a similar method to attack full court zone presses. He called it "4-up." Instead of my alignment, he had the four players inbounds line up four across facing the player out-of-bounds for the throw-in. The two guards line up inside the other two with one each where the foul line intersects the foul lane. The other two are spaced one each in the outside lanes of the court, right and left of the guards. This gives you a 4-up line across the court.

His system used a strategy identical to mine of always having a guard in the middle as the ball is advanced up the court versus the press. It all hinges on who receives the first pass, or if the ball is reversed after the first pass as to who cuts where. It seems to work very efficiently as well as mine. Mostly, the first pass can be more successfully thrown to one of the outside receivers, rather than a guard. Teams do not pressure these players as tightly as the guards. Your choice as to which initial alignment to use. Both works.

CHAPTER 16

SWISH... HOW TO PUT A ROUND BALL THROUGH AN ORANGE CIRCLE

SHOOTING! Walk into any gym. There is a basketball laying on the floor. A youngster is with you. They will walk or run over to the ball, pick it up, bounce it once or twice and shoot. If it goes "swish" through the net, they will probably smile and yell with glee. The same display of satisfaction happens regardless of the age of the shooter. I have observed it many times. Shooting basketballs is fun. Putting them through the orange circle is a double pleasure. That is the main objective of basketball. Score to win and you must shoot to score. I have a separate chapter devoted to shooting because it is the "biggie" of basketball offensive skills and demands hours and hours of practice to better.

Be advised that when you have players who lack shooting, do not expect them to improve rapidly, even with expert coaching. I read a short synopsis of a book titled, "Shooting the Rock," by authors, Gary Boren, Mark Mason, and Denny Price. They made a significant statement that has remained with me. It was, "The greatest of all faults is to imagine that you have none. Lessons are not to take the place of practice, but to make practice worthwhile." How true that is! A student must be coachable, willing to listen, accept change, and most of all, practice the good habits, and not repeat the old ones. This applies to coaches and teachers as well.

Personally, I am a decent golfer, and I make that statement modestly to make an analogous point. Very often people have requested me to aid them with their game. I have done so with pleasure. One of the most important things I relate to them is to understand muscles have to be trained, and that takes time. That means practice and hours of it. I say, "I cannot unscrew the top of one's head and pour this data into your brain and automatically your muscles will respond." Professionally, golfers spend countless hours practicing golf skills to maintain their proficiency in their trade. Some call it muscle-memory. Thus, it is mandatory for whomever I am attempting to help to leave me and go practice the changes I have passed on to them. This is a must to achieve improvement.

It is the same with shooting skills. You may coach a player and give them advice which changes their shooting style. This player must now proceed on their own and practice these new suggestion(s). The player has to break away from an old muscle habit and create a new one. Not as easy as it sounds. Much easier for the newer or younger player to the game, than one who has had no teachings or is self-taught. Habits do not change on their own or are "wished away." One has to work diligently and consistently to establish new habits. Work for the basketball player is practice. Lots of it. Then, gradually new muscle-memory is established.

Like all basketball offensive skills, there are fundamentally right ways to shoot the basketball. Of course, there are always exceptions to every rule. I used to jokingly tell my players concerning free throw shooting, "If you can make a high percentage by closing your eyes and stand on one foot, continue this method." My point being, if you are having problems shooting from the foul line, please change. Exceptions are few and far between. Therefore, if your players are not being successful, insist and even force them to change to better fundamentals that you will show them.

The main fundamental of shooting the basketball is the ability to shoot it straight. Even small deviations from this greatly reduces the shooter's success rate. Next is the arc of flight of the ball toward the goal. If you ask players, "Where are you aiming the ball? What is your target?" You will get different replies. "The rim," "The front of the rim," "The basket," "Just over the front rim," or no response, just a shrug of the shoulders.

Yes, it is possible to make a shot that just clears the front rim. It is also possible to make a shot where the ball has a much higher arc and clears the front rim by a greater margin. That is what a good shot is and one that you want for your players. The margin of error is decreased with high arcing shots from any distance. High arcing shots do not always go "swish," but have a better chance of still going in, even if they hit the rim first. Often a good shooter gets the "shooters bounce." High arcing shot is a slower shot as gravity slows its flight toward the goal. Flat shots are fast, quick, and more forceful shots in their route to the goal. Not what a good shooter wants. Therefore, shoot straight with a high arcing flight, and smile when it goes in. Here are a few fundamental skills to impart to your players. For free throw shots:

1. Is the ball traveling straight? Check shooting forearm. It should form a right angle with the upper arm and be directly under the ball.
2. Is the arc high enough to get the ball entering the basket nearer the back of the rim than the front?
3. Knees flexed enough to get the "power" to get the ball to the basket. The shot starts in the legs.
4. Ball should be resting on the finger pads of the shooting hand, not the palm.
5. Use as little movement of the ball prior to release as possible. Excessive movement increases errors.
6. To release, flex the knees upward to begin the shot. As the shooting arm extends fully upward to release the ball in a flowing

motion over the fore and middle fingers by "goose necking" the wrist at release and follow through. Should be a unified, flowing motion of all parts. Not jerky or flipping motion with the wrist or fingers.

For Jump Shots:
1. Square the body and shoot to the basket.
2. Do not drift left, right forward or backward. Return to the floor in the approximate spot from where you jumped from.
3. Proper release and follow through as in the free throw shot.
4. Shoot straight with sufficient arc.
5. Know your effective range, have confidence. Quick release.

I have given you some of the necessary skills to teach in shooting the basketball. While on that subject, here are some simple drills to aid that cause. You could include these in your daily station drills format.

1. Have players pair off with a ball a few feet apart. The player with the ball will now "shoot" the ball into the air as they would in taking a shot at the basket. The shooter is to check out the backspin on the ball. Also, to exaggerate the follow through by extending the elbow of the shooting arm whereby the wrist ends in a "gooseneck" downward

position from the fully extended arm. Hold the follow through until the partner catches the ball. Now the partner "shoots" the ball back to the partner as they shot the ball to them.

2. Another variation of doing this drill is to give each player a ball and have them "shoot" in the air. They are to hold the follow through until the ball hits the floor. Retrieve the ball and repeat.

3. Another version is to have players with a ball stand in front of a wall. They repeatedly "shoot" the ball against the wall, emulating a shot.

All these drills aid the shooters to improve the proper release of the ball with a high arc and with a good follow through. Remember, you are teaching new habits. My son Michael and I would attend the University of North Carolina's Dean Smith summer basketball camps. I believe he was nine years old when he started. He attended for about five summers. He went on to play high school basketball at the Gilman School in Baltimore. There he set the school record for the most points scored in a single game with 48. Without the three-point line, that record still stands after almost 40 years. Michael went on to play at Johns Hopkins University. To this day, I credit the shooting drills he did at a young age at UNC's summer camps for his ability to be an incredibly good "shooter of the rock."

CHAPTER 17

MISCELLANEOUS DRILLS

To successfully teach basketball properly, you must do so using various drills, each emphasizing some necessary phase of the game. If you have ever taken any type of mathematics class, the instructor did not merely stand before the students and explain how they should solve math problems. They were assigned math problems to solve in order to better understand "how" and "why." It is the same with basketball skills. The coach talks about certain situations that always arise in a basketball game. Then, they drill the players so they can improve their skill levels in order to be better.

The definition of drill: "A physical or mental exercise aimed at perfecting facility and skill... the approved or correct procedure for accomplishing something efficiently." "Learning takes place more efficiently when drills are practiced repeatedly in short time segments... repetition is a vital necessity... again, it is repetition, repetition, repetition." To summarize, choose drills that are calculated to aid in improving a basketball skill. Include drills in every daily practice schedule. Make these drills short in duration. Though short, repeat them often and add as you deem necessary. Some drills you may use all season. I have listed many of the drills I used during my career. I noted, as I researched my past practice schedules, that some were used career long. I assumed that these "did the job." I hope you find a few that accomplish this for you.

I state herewith that some were originated by me. However, the source for most was through book or magazine research, or from basketball clinic speakers. Sometimes I added or subtracted from the original to suit our teams' needs.

Here is a short list of drills that I feel can make your players better. These are in addition to the many I have described in previous chapters. Note that I have named each drill. I did this to save you time by not having to detail each drill to the players when you repeat it in the next or future practices.

1. P-D-R- The "P" stands for passer; the "D" stands for defender; the "R" stands for receiver. Formation of the drill; two lines in single file facing each other with the first player in one line with a basketball. They are the first passer. That person is closely

guarded by another player, the defender, and the first person in the other line is the receiver. The passer's task is to successfully complete a pass to the receiver as the defender does all in his power to prevent this. No lob passes allowed. After the passer makes the pass, they rush to defend against the receiver of the pass, thus becoming the new defender against the new passer. The new receiver is the next person in line after the pass is made. Once a pass is made, the defender goes to the end of the line of the passer and the drill continues. Divide your squad into as many lines as you wish to get more done in the quickest amount of practice time.

  XXXPD   RRRRXXX

To vary the drill, put the defender away from the passer about halfway between the passer and the receiver. Now the passer must dribble up to defender, stop dribbling and then pass to the receiver. The passer than remains in place to become the new defender while the new receiver dribbles up to them. Continue the drill.

    XXXP   D   RRRRXXX

2.   Four Ball Shooting - I used this drill all season as my pregame warm up drill as well as in

daily practices. You can get a lot of shooting practice done in a short amount of time. This includes layups and jump shots. Divide your squad in half. One single file line at midcourt circle with four basketballs, one each in the hands of the first four players. Position the other half at the right at midcourt where the half-court line intersects the sideline. Put one player on the foul line, facing the first player with a ball at midcourt. To begin, the first player with a ball passes to the player facing him on the foul line. As the pass is being made, the first player to the right cuts hard to the basket for a pass to shoot a layup shot. After the shot, the shooter continues up the court to receive a pass from the rebounder and joins the passing line at mid-court with the ball. The rebounder, after the shot and his pass to the shooter continuing up-court, turns and goes up-court along the sideline to the shooting line. The rebounder at the foul line is replaced by the passer who made the initial pass to the rebounder, and the drill continues.

3. Bull(s) in the Ring - This is a good drill to teach players to see the court for open receivers as they are being closely defended and a possible interceptor is nearby. Put your squad in a circle formation. One player is given a basketball and is closely guarded by

another. Put another player in the center of the circle. The object of the player with the ball is to complete a successful pass to anyone else on the circle except a player next to them. No lob passes allowed. For the player in the middle of the circle to get out of the circle, they must deflect a pass, cause the passer to make a bad pass or intercept a pass. That player replaces the player who made the mistake, and the drill continues. For variety, put two players in the middle and one closely guarding. If the pass is successful, the center player closest to the receiver of the pass now goes quickly to closely guard that player. The player who was guarding the passer now becomes an interceptor in the middle. If a player makes a mistake, they must get in the circle as an interceptor.

NOTE: If you want to practice passing out of a double team as in a pressing defense, in both the P-D-R drill and the BULL(s) in the Ring drills, do what I called "Closing the Gate." Whenever a receiver catches a pass, have the player on each side of them, double team that player aggressively. In the P-D-R drill you have to designate and rotate the double teamers. Same rules apply for mistakes and changing player duties.

    4. Pressure Layup - This drill is a good one to teach players to dribble-drive hard to the basket for a layup shot after obtaining the

ball in open court either by an interception, steal, loose ball, or a pass from a teammate. Typically, when this occurs, a defender will be hustling after the dribbler to hopefully prevent a score. Often, the dribbler will be glancing over his shoulder instead of looking straight ahead. Also, they will attempt to avoid getting fouled with some off balance shot attempt as the basket is reached. Instruct the dribbler to aggressively go up for the layup shot in a realistic fashion to at least get fouled, make the layup or maybe both. Here is the drill formation.

Start with two lines. One starting on the foul line block and the second starting in the middle right outside fast break lane even with an imaginary line drawn through the top of the foul circle to the sideline. This outside line has the basketballs, at least four. The first player in line begins a right-hand speed dribble toward the basket at the far end of the court. The first player in the other line waits until the dribbler takes a couple of dribbles, then sprints to get to the dribbler as fast as they can. The dribbler is to get to the basket as fast as possible for a layup without paying any attention to the efforts of the defender attempting to catch up. Once the action at the far basket is completed, the second players in the lines repeat the drill. The completed players switch lines at the far end and repeat the drill coming back to the near end. Thus, you have continuous action at both baskets. To practice a left-handed speed dribble, merely stop action and move the lines to the corresponding areas of the court on the other side.

Points of emphasis of the drill are:
a. The dribbler uses the proper hand to speed dribble.
b. Dribbler gets to the basket as efficiently as possible without concern for the trailing defender.
c. Shooter attempts a "normal" layup despite the aggressiveness of the trailer.
d. The trailer does all possible to pressure the shooter.

5. Reverse Pivot & Block Out - Many coaches "talk" blocking out and rebounding, but spend very little time in properly teaching this skill. Here is a simple drill I used to teach this fundamental. The first part to teach is the Reverse Pivot. You will be amazed just how many will not know how to perform this defensive rebounding skill. This includes not only how, but merely what a reverse pivot is.

Here is a brief synopsis of what usually occurs when a shot is attempted. The offensive players who will be the rebounders, will move quickly to do so. They will either go to the right or the left of the defender guarding them. Here is where the reverse pivot is essential. If the offensive player goes to the left of his defender, the defender MUST pivot on their left foot and swing the body in a reverse motion so their back blocks the path of the rebounder. When the rebounder goes right, pivot on the right and swing the body in a reverse motion. DO NOT ALLOW THE DEFENDER TO USE A FRONT PIVOT AND ATTEMPT TO STEP IN FRONT OF THE OFFENSIVE PLAYER. Usually this prevents a proper block out and often, causes a personal foul.

To teach the reverse pivot, merely line your players beside each other with spacing. As coach, face them so all can see. Now, demonstrate a reverse pivot. Use another coach or another player to aid you. Have this aide "walk" past you to your right and then to your left. Each time illustrate the proper footwork and body movement to reverse pivot. After this demonstration, stand in front of the line of players and face them. Instruct them that when you raise your right arm, or merely point, the rebounder is going to their left. Now each player must reverse pivot in that direction. Do the same with the left arm. Now each player must reverse pivot to their right. Repeat this preliminary for a practice or two until you feel confident that they have mastered it.

Then, divide your squad into two even lines, facing each other as demonstrated below. The coach will stand behind one line in a position where that line cannot see them.

To drill, the coach will point or raise their right or left arm to indicate to the players in the line facing them which gap to cut through to rebound. The defender must reverse pivot properly to prevent the rebounder from advancing further. To allow all to be a defender, the coach merely walks through the formation to a position where the "Ds" become "Os" and continue. Watch carefully to see all players reverse pivot correctly. Note: Allow some rough play as you decide.

Sometimes a potential rebounder will not advance toward the basket after a shot attempt, but merely stands in place. Often this is a smaller player and not a consistent rebounder. Teach your players when this happens, they should step forward at this player, make legal contact, and go rebound the ball. This way your team is blocking out all five opponents. As I stated in an earlier chapter, "Playing good defense is necessary, but defensive rebounding is the final step!" Do not take this skill for granted. It must be drilled.

6. IN THE SOUP - This is a drill I used to emphasize defense when we were outnumbered by opponents in a fast break or break away. The in the

soup denotes the player or players on defense as the offensive players are advancing to score. Start with a 2-on-1 situation. The defensive player is stationed on the foul line area as two offensive players come at them to score. The object of the "soup" defender is to cause a mistake by the offense, i.e., bad pass, fumble, missed pass, too many passers, a bad or missed shot, etc. If that defender is successful, they are replaced by the player who erred. If the offense is successful, the soup player remains on defense until an error is caused.

The next step is the 3-on-2 situation. It is necessary to teach first the proper techniques for the defenders to use. I always taught the defenders to line up in tandem. One in front at the top of the foul circle and the other behind in the foul lane. The top player was not to allow dribble penetration and to cause the dribbler to make a mistake. Once the dribbler made the first pass, the rule was to drop quickly to the opposite block to prevent a pass from the initial offensive receiver to a cutting player and then to the basket. Also, if the top player caused a quick jump shot, their job was successful. The bottom defender's rule was to go quickly in the direction of the first pass from the middle dribbler. That player was to prevent penetration and a resulting layup. If that offensive player made a pass back to the top, the opposite defender returned as best as possible to harass a potential jump shot. If the defenders can cause several passes, this gives the other teammates a chance to get back to help. Again, the players "in the soup" stay on defense until an offensive mistake is committed. This drill also aids your offense passing, ball-handling, and shooting. Therefore, though a defensive drill, be sure to commend or coach as needed to both the defensive players and offensive.

Here are my last comments for this chapter. They have to do with conditioning. Most coaches will conclude practice with wind sprints and I certainly did as well. For variety, use these conditioning drills as well.

A. Lateral Line Jumps - Have each of your team members select a line on the court, usually the side lines, but any line is OK. Instruct each player turn sideways to the line, bending their knees slightly and together. On your signal, have them jump laterally back and forth over the line as low and as fast as possible. They are not to jump high, but to stay as low as possible to clear the line. They continue until you give a stop signal, usually a whistle.

B. Shuttle Run - Basketball is a game of running back and forth with stops and starts in a confined area with quickness. In this drill, split your squad in half. Get each half to line up on a sideline, facing a foul circle. On a whistle signal from you, have them shuttle run as fast as possible to the foul line circle, touch the circle line and return to touch the sideline. Continue this with quickness until you whistle them to cease.

C. Change of Direction - This drill is a variation of the wind sprints. As I mentioned, basketball is a game of changing situations. For example, your team is in the midst of fast breaking, and a pass is intercepted by the opponents. Immediately, your five players must change direction and get back on defense. Here is a game-like drill. Split your squad in half as to run wind sprints by groups. Station one half at one end behind the baseline and the other half behind the first group. On your whistle, the first group begins sprinting to the far end of the court. If a whistle blows during the sprint, they stop and reverse direction back to the area court-wide below the foul line, turn, and run in place. When the whistle blows, they once again begin sprinting to the other baseline. If a whistle does not sound, they continue towards the other end, touch the baseline, turn, and begin sprinting back. Every time a whistle blows during the sprinting, players change direction and retreat to the area past the foul line. There they run in place until the whistle blows again. Continue as long as you see fit. Then bring the second group on court and repeat as you did with the first group.

This drill is more game-like and breaks the monotony of robot-like running back and forth. It is somewhat like the shuttle run drill, though a longer area. Keep them guessing as to when the whistle is going to sound and have them hustle every second they are on the court.

In summary, let me emphasize there are literally a multitude of valuable drills for one to research and possibly implement for use with your team. Do so and select those that will aid the skills of your squad. I have merely listed some that I feel abetted my teams over the years. "Little things mean a lot!" Not just in relationships, but teaching is essential to good coaching, and hopefully winning games. Therefore, analyze your team's weaknesses carefully and use drills to aid your personnel to improve. Do not merely give lip service. Action speaks much louder than words. DRILL, DRILL, DRILL!

CHAPTER 18

DEFENSIVE NUMBERING SYSTEM

If you choose to use multiple defenses, you will need a method to communicate quickly and simply to your players what defense you desire for them to utilize at any given moment during a game. Additionally, before the start of a game, at the end of quarters, at half time or during all time-outs. Time is precious in these situations. An efficient, uncomplicated procedure is necessary to communicate to your team what defense you want and when. The best, in my opinion, is a numbering system. With this type, you call out a number and your team know instantly how you desire them to defend.

I will list my suggestions below, and they are numerous. By no means am I saying that you use them all. Pick and choose to suit your needs and adjust accordingly.

Preface: single digit number is a half-court defense. Double digit number is a full court defense. If digits are different, first digit indicates defense for offensive backcourt, and second digit indicates defense for offensive frontcourt.

NUMBER	TYPE OF DEFENSE
1	½ court pressure man-to-man
11	Full court pressure man-to-man
2	½ court 2-3 (2-1-2) zone
22	full court 2-3 (2-1-2) zone press
3	½ court 1-3-1 zone
33	full court 1-3-1 zone press
4	½ court 3-2 (1-2-2) zone
44	full court 3-2 (1-2-2) zone press
5	½ court zone press, trapping on every pass in offensive front court
55	2-1-2 alignment then force up the sidelines and trap as in #5 above
12	full court man-to-man; ½ court #2 zone
13	full court man-to-man; ½ #3 zone
14	full court man-to-man; ½ court #4
21	full court 2-1-2 zone; ½ court man-to-man
31	full court 1-3-1 zone; ½ court man-to-man

41	full court 3-2 zone; ½ court man-to-man
0	guards only ½ court man-to-man; 3-man ½ court zone triangle
00	guards only full court man-to-man; 3-man ½ court zone triangle

Note: in numbers 22, 33, & 44, I did not double team or trap. This can be optional. Additionally, we used 00 & 0 very sparingly. They are defenses used for very special situations.

As an added twist, a letter may be added to defensive number as follows:

LETTER DEFINITION

S	Blitz switch. Can be used with any man-to-man
T	Automatic double team traps in ½ court zone defenses (2,3,4) when offense passes ball to baseline areas.
X	Defense begins in one ½ court defense than switches to another. (example:23X — begin in #2 zone and adjust to #3 zone; 21X — begin #2 zone and adjust to man-to-man.
H	Move ½ court zone defenses out farther (higher) from the baseline and basket area. (2H, 3H, 4H)

| B | Box and one (4-man zone & 1 man-to-man) |
| D | Diamond and one (4-man zone & 1 man-to-man) |

I have listed a total of 24 defenses. Too many for a young, inexperienced team to master and too many for most any team to include in their defensive repertoire. I listed them because we used some form of them over the years at one time or another, and a few just for a special situation. Therefore, do not get "greedy." Teach the basics. A strong man-to-man foundation, some solid zones and only add the extras when you honestly feel your team can handle the "adjustments" adequately enough to be successful. As I reiterated in an earlier chapter, "it is not the number of defenses your team has in its playbook, it is the number it can play well!" DO NOT ATTEMPT TO PLAY ANY DEFENSE FOR ANY LENGTH OF TIME IN A GAME UNLESS YOU HAVE SPENT PRACTICE TIME WITH IT! I believe the results will be harmful if you do. Stick with the known and the reliable.

Hopefully, this chapter will present to you what is possible defensively. Once again, teaching defense is work and time consuming to achieve maximum results. Let a word to the wise be sufficient, choose intelligently.

CHAPTER 19

SPECIAL SITUATIONS & DIVERSE MINUTIA

The actual game of basketball is filled with special situations that call for a coach's answer or adjustment. I wrote in Chapter 3, "Qualifications of a coach," a recommendation. Before the start of any season, make two all-inclusive lists, one for offense and one for defense. These lists should include any game situation that might arise for your team during the course of any game. Here are some which will need your practice attention.

1. Out-of-Bounds with the Ball
   The referee's whistle is blown many, many times as the game progresses. If the whistle means your team will gain possession of the ball out-of-bounds for a throw-in, how will your team be able to do this, especially if the opponents exert defensive pressure? You

must practice alignments from the sidelines, from the baseline under your basket, and to advance the ball the entire length of the court. Note, I have included in Chapter 12 one extensive method on how to beat the full court zone press defense. I had much success using the offense explained there.

If you have the ball on the baseline at your basket, then you have the option of many alignments to score quickly with a set "play" that you have designed. There are scores of these. Research and select for your team's abilities.

If you have a throw-in from the sidelines, remember to teach your players ALL such throw-ins are of the spot type; meaning your player cannot move sidewards from the designated spot for the throw-in. A violation like this is a loss of the ball. This can be very costly in a close game.

2. Opponent's Ball Out-of-Bounds

I described three places in #1 above where the ball may be taken out-of-bounds. The sidelines, under the basket or to be taken the length of the court. Let us talk about under the basket first. Here, usually the opponents will attempt an alignment that will get them a quick shot for a score. To counteract, you must decide what defense you will play, zone or man-to-man. Many teams will decide to play zone to avoid various cuts and screens in a congested area. This decision is not always the answer. If this is your choice, make sure you teach your players how to play defense in a zone. Particularly if you are mostly a man-to-man team. Otherwise, you will find your opponent getting high percentage shots after the throw-in.

Now, with the other two areas, sidelines and length of the court, there are variables to consider. What has been your defense? What is the score? How much time remains in the game? What is the foul situation with your team? Do you want to pressure? How successful is my present defense? There is no definitive answer. It will depend on the game circumstances and what you deem the best at the time.

3. Fouling on Purpose

   Several years ago, North Carolina State upset Georgetown University in the final game of the NCAA tournament to win the national championship. Jim Valvano, State's head coach, gave instructions to his team when they fell several points behind to foul intentionally on every possession of Georgetown. His strategy worked as Georgetown failed to convert enough free throws to hold their lead and State won the game on a rebound shot in the final second.

You see this plan in motion in all games on every level these days. The trailing team does not always win as State did, but sometimes they do: a big reason to practice this scenario. When doing so, instruct your players to make a valid attempt to go for the ball in fouling. I used to have a verbal signal when I wanted my team to foul on purpose. It was "RED," and I would shout it if needed.

If you are aware of who on the opposing team is their target to receive the throw-in, it is a good idea to tell your team to do all in their power to prevent this person from receiving the ball because that player is their best foul shooter. Not always easy, but worth the effort. If there is very little time remaining, another strategy is to foul a player before the throw-in. This way no time runs off the clock. Also, it solves the dilemma of their best shooter getting the ball.

4. Time Clock Strategy and Taking the "Last Shot"

   The game time clock is always a factor to consider, especially during a closely contested game. Every ball possession is critical in these types of games and "time and situation" have to be considered by you, the coach. I recounted in an earlier chapter how my team in one crucial championship game versus a superior, undefeated team, maintained possession of the ball for seven continual minutes prior to the end of the first half. This would not be possible in college games now because of the time clock to shoot. However, in boys' high school games, there is no time clock to shoot. I believe this is true also in most recreational and club games. Therefore, if you are coaching on any of the latter levels, clock strategy is an item that must be included on your "to practice list."

There are four quarters in each game. That means there will be four times in every game that the clock will show less than one minute to play in that quarter, half, or end of game. You, as coach, must make two separate decisions. When to begin to take the last shot and who do you want to take it. The first decision will often vary because of the present circumstances of the game, i.e., what is the score, how strong is your opponent, are you satisfied with how your team is contesting. To satisfy the second decision, I always had in our offensive arsenal, last shot options within the offensive pattern we used. Many times, near the end of my practice, I would set up a time remaining and score condition to practice against various defenses. This practice often came in handy as we faced a crucial point in a game. Practice does not always make perfect, but it sure helps when your team must attempt to score. Otherwise, a wild, low percentage try is the last resort and most likely a turnover.

5. Defensive Free Throws Specials

    Your opponents have been awarded either a 1-and-1 or two free throws. At selected times in the game, you may want to spring a surprise when the last shot is successful. Let's suppose that your team has leisurely taken the ball out-of-bounds, tossed in bounds and slowly advanced the ball up court to this point. Here is the surprise. My teams had a designed play which I called 52 or 43. I will explain the numbers. On a free throw, the non-shooting team is given the inside positions along the foul lane. On the right side was my #5 player and on the left was #4. #2 was on the side with #4 and #3 on the side with #5. #1 was outside the foul circle behind the shooter. If we called 52, #5 would rebound the ball as it came through the nets, catching it without letting it hit the floor, then hurrying out-of-bounds at the baseline, and passing the ball to #2 as they step quickly backwards toward their sideline. #3 blocks out the shooter and then races to the midcourt area in front of #2. #4 does not interfere with the ball as it comes through the nets for #5. Instead, they sprint down the left side of the court toward the left block at the other basket.

When #2 catches the ball, they immediately pass to #3 at midcourt. #1 sprints up the middle as a possible receiver. When #3 gets the ball, they attack with a dribble down the right side of the court. If properly executed, now your team has an advantage with #4 on the left block, #1 in the middle and #3 attacking from the right. If the path to the basket is clear, #3 advances with their dribble as far as they can. If #1 is open in the middle, they should pass to them and continue cutting to the right block. With #1 having the ball, your 3-on-2 develops as planned. One other coaching point, as #3 is advancing on the right and they see #1 is covered defensively, they should dribble toward the foul circle instead of the right block. When they do, #1 now cuts behind #3 and curls to the right block, still giving you the desired 3-on-2 effect with the ball in the middle.

If we call 43, roles are reversed as we will take the break down the left side of the court. #4 rebounds the made shot as it passes through the net; #5 leaves the ball alone and sprints down the right side of the court to the right block at the other basket; #3 steps quickly backwards toward their sideline; #2 blocks out the shooter and sprints to the midcourt in front of #3; #1 is outside the foul circle behind the shooter; #4 grabs the ball from the net, sprints left outside the baseline and passes quickly to #3; #3 looks up court and passes to #2 at midcourt; #1 cuts up the middle as a possible receiver. When #2 gets the ball, if their path to the basket is clear, they advance the ball as far as they can. If #1 is open in the middle, they should pass to them and continue cutting toward the block on the left. As with play 52, you have the desired 3-on-2 situation with 43. #3 and #4 follow up-court to the left and right elbow areas respectively for the secondary fast break and possible shots if we do not get one with the initial three players, #5, #2 and #1.

These "specials" are easy to drill and do not use much practice time. We usually did so near the end of the session. It was worth it because during the seasons we scored numerous points utilizing these free throw plays.

While we are discussing defensive free throw situations, I want to pass on a couple more practical hints. I have seen and heard many coaches yell to their players just prior to an opponent shooting a free throw, "Block Out!" Let me emphasize, "Players have to be taught how to properly block out during free throws." The major mistake the defensive players closest to the basket make is they step forward into the lane, causing them to be too far under the basket. Often the result is the missed shot bounces over their head into the hands of an offensive player. The best mechanics to teach is to have your inside players STEP OVER and make block out contact with the offensive player next to them. They should have their feet spread and their hands up in the order to catch the possible missed shot. If the other two teammates on the foul lane STEP OVER as well, you now have the two offensive players along the lane "pinched in." This makes it exceedingly difficult for them to rebound.

Here is another circumstance that arises in the final seconds of a close game. The defensive team on the foul lane is behind by one, two or three points, a one possession situation. Many coaches instruct their rebounder to call an immediate time out as soon as they catch the ball. This means the team will have to go the full length of the court after a throw-in from the baseline to obtain a possible shot to tie or win the game. Personally, I always had a different philosophy for this predicament. If the opponents had the free throw shooter, two others on the foul lane, and remaining two back on defense, I would instruct my team to rebound and fast break as best they could to get the last shot. This way the opponents are not in a five-person set defense but scrambling to get back as we advance the ball. I felt this gave us a better chance at an open, high percentage shot. We did not always make the shot, but many times we got the shot.

I told you in an earlier chapter how we won an important championship game with a miraculous midcourt shot. I relate another about rebounding a missed free throw and not calling time. We were playing a junior college team, who had never beaten us. However, with about six minutes to play, we were 15 points behind. It was one of those games where my leading scorer was having an "off" day shooting, we had several questionable officials' calls go against us, the ball was not bouncing our way, and it appeared as though it was a game we were not going to win. In fact, I remember saying to my assistant after we were trailing by those 15 points, "I am not sure we are going to win this one." An assumption I rarely had. Well, we began to turn up the "heat" defensively and made some shots. The result was with 10 seconds to go we trailed by two points, and an opponent was on the foul line with a 1-and-1. They again missed the first shot and my rebounder caught the ball this time, and passed quickly to my point guard, who was directly in front of our bench some

65 or 70 feet away from our basket. The guard turned and threw a baseball-like shot at our goal. IT WENT IN! Miracles of Miracles! If we had called time out on that last rebound, we would not have won that game.

6. Preseason Try-Outs and Reducing the Squad
As early November arrives, football season is drawing to a close and many begin thinking about round ball season. If this is your first season as a head basketball coach, for certain you must have a plan for preseason try-outs. I remember vividly my initial season at Baltimore City College in 1960. At the time, City was a large, all-male high school. Presently, its enrollment is not as huge, and it is co-ed. The athletic program included three levels of basketball; freshmen-sophomore, junior varsity, and varsity. Each had its own coach and schedule. During the fall season as I scouted about for potential players in the school and my physical education classes, I discovered this dilemma. In past years, players would pick and choose as to which of the three teams they would try out for. Also, juniors were permitted to play on the junior varsity. Only freshmen and sophomores were allowed on that level team. Each level had its own separate try-outs. My decision at the outset answer to all was, "Everyone tries out for the VARSITY!" We

coaches, then would determine who would play on which team.

When I scheduled my first meeting in the school auditorium of all interested candidates, over 300 showed up! Yes, 300! Briefly, I will relate how we faced and solved that problem. We scheduled practices in divided shifts. We had each player wear a white tee shirt with his last name printed on his back for quick identification purposes. I really do no recall exactly how many days it took, but it was not as many as you might think to reduce to workable numbers. I will explain later some of the drills we used. After the first season when we started winning, the numbers reduced each year as we built our teams mostly from returnees of the previous year, though the freshmen team was the exception. They were new to the school, but they always had to try-out so, I, the varsity coach could see them perform. The system worked as all three teams won championships: the varsity four times in eight seasons.

Many coaches use scrimmage as the main way to size up candidates and reduce the squad. I used it minimally because I felt that a player's fundamental skill level was more important. Those fundamental skills are dribbling, passing, passing on the move, catching, and shooting. Therefore, I recommend you set up drills that emphasize these necessary abilities. In this manner, you see each individual's deftness. In a scrimmage, a player may rarely get the ball to shoot, a pass to catch, a chance to dribble etc. Sometimes instead of playing 5-on-5, we would reduce teams to 3-on-3, or even 1-on-1. This method gives you a more definitive evaluation of each person.

I was never too quick with the trigger to cut the squad. Do not misunderstand, if the numbers are large and your time is limited, you will have to hasten. Usually, I found that an excessively big number could be reduced in short order. However, once we were down to workable size, I wanted to make very sure that I did not make mistakes in cutting. When in doubt, I always was slow to make the final decision on some players.

Truthfully, some players cut themselves. Why? First of all, they discover that practices are hard work with a lot of running and nothing like the "pick-up" games on the sandlots. Then, there are coaches who tell them what is acceptable and what is not. They are being disciplined and instructed. They decide, this is not for me and stop coming to practices. Occasionally, a candidate will inform you that they did not realize how time consuming being on a team could be. Hence, they quit. Of course, eventually you will have to decide on who will be your final group and cut some. This is one of the most distasteful tasks of a coach, informing some "they did not make the team."

You may be wondering, "How many players did I keep to make up my squad?" If you are the head varsity coach, to me 12 or 13 was sort of the perfect number. A couple of seasons, I did retain 15. I believe this is too many because the game is only 32 minutes and it is exceedingly difficult to give sufficient playing to 15.

Believe me, PT (playing time) is important and on the minds of every team member. Maybe not so much at the very beginning of the season as enthusiasm and excitement in making the team is rampant. However, these feelings subside quickly, particularly if your team is not winning as expected. Your bench players, the ones not getting a lot of game time, become itchy, discontented, and even rebellious. "Why is he playing ahead of me? Why doesn't the coach like me? Why? Why? Why?" Now you have a morale problem. Some parents will question you as to why their child is not playing more. This is never a pleasant situation and certainly not conducive to teamwork or a necessary unselfish attitude by all. I really never had these problems as my teams were highly successful. All enjoy being a winner, not so much a loser.

If you are an under-squad coach, JV, middle school, 10-12, 13-15, club or recreational, I believe you can keep a larger number of players, 14-16. The object of these types of teams is to concentrate on teaching beginning players. Yes, all want to win games, but it should not be the sole object.

CHAPTER 20

SOME OFF THE COURT NECESSARY ITEMS

It is mid-summer and you have just been appointed to your first head basketball coaching position. Before you are over your elation and celebration, the beginning of the season will be upon you. There are several necessary details you must prepare preseason.

To begin, know where you will have your practices. When can you begin? What time of day or evening? How long do you have the facility each practice session? Is there a rule against length of practices and what days are permissible? When does the regular season start? Is the upcoming regular season and preseason scrimmages schedule complete?

Other necessities to know include, will you have the use of the practice area alone or with another group? If possible, I strongly urge that you acquire the facility alone. That way, you have the full court area. After all, the game is played full court and you definitely will need the opportunity to practice full court fundamentals. When alone, you will be the only voice heard to acquire the strict attention of your players. No doubt, you will be able to get more accomplished in the time allotted as well. The noise factor and avid inattention to the coach always hinder any positive learning. Other factors to consider are, is the scoreboard in good working order? Will you need keys to open locked doors or turn on lights?

Some auxiliary or supplementary personnel will be needed by you in subsidiary roles. The first would be an assistant coach. Choose this person wisely. Select someone who can be present on a regular basis; one who has a similar philosophy as yours; one you feel can be loyal; one you feel can creditably coach the team in your absence. If they are inexperienced, it is vital for you to teach them as you proceed. Emphasize your philosophy. Always explain your reasoning for coaching techniques and what you expect from your players to your assistant.

You will need a team manager. This is a student who can attend practices and games consistently. Duties may be varied, such as, making sure all needed equipment is available prior to start of home practices and stored afterwards. They would also make sure said equipment, like balls and first aid kits, are ready for transport for all away games and scrimmages. Additionally, the manager should see to it that towels and water are available at the bench area during games. Any other minor duties may be assigned or determined by you.

Two other valuable assistants to your program are a keeper of the score book and an operator of the game clock. If possible, I recommend adults for both tasks. If not, please train two students for these two duties. Both are crucial to an error free and smooth function of a game. The home scorebook is always designated prior to start of the game by the head referee as the official book of the contest. There is tangible information in each score book to include the running score, time outs, and individual personal fouls. If a disagreement arises between the information in the home score book and the visitor's, the home book recording is the official one. With this onus on the scorekeepers, train yours well!

The timer must be sufficiently instructed in operating the official game clock. There are specific rules as to when the clock starts and stops, and when a substitute is allowed to enter the game. Usually, the head referee will review these rules with the timer prior to the start of the game. However, train your timer thoroughly. A scoring error or timing mistake could make a big difference in a closely contested game. These two adjunct officials should be a great aid to the court game officials to assure that every game is played without controversy.

You may choose to elicit some other helpers in your program. They would be statisticians. These are usually students who record usable and valuable information about each player who participates in a game. This data usually includes field goal attempts (both two & three pointers), made field goals, offensive and defensive, rebounds, steals, interceptions and offensive turnovers. Most likely, you will have to tutor these volunteers as to the specifics and definition of each statistic. As an aside, sometimes I would ask a player who got cut from the squad during preseasons, if they would like to help the team in any of these auxiliary jobs. Often, they would.

If you are employed in a school system, most likely you will be required to obtain a completed physician's physical examination form from each player prior to the first practice. In addition, those same players are to be given a permission form for their parents or guardian to sign, granting approval for their child to participate in your program. I would also suggest this procedure if you were to coach in a non-school program, such as a recreational or club activity. If the school has a medical person on staff, be sure to arrange with that person a schedule of physical exams for your candidates well in advance of your initial practice. Do not allow any player participation without a medical exam and parental permission. You could be inviting possible legal problems if you do.

Be sure to issue advance notice for all prospective players to see or hear about your initial meeting for them to attend. At this meeting, you pass on to them personal information forms, medical forms, and parent permission slips. Wise to set a future date for these forms to be returned to you, especially the medical exam and parental permission forms. NO FORMS -

NO PARTICIPATION! At this first meeting, it is also a good time to inform prospects of ways to get in better physical condition for basketball, particularly their legs and feet. Early pulled muscles and blistered feet hinder their ability to practice and make the team.

Once the squad is selected, schedule a meeting of player's parents or guardians. Pass out the seasonal schedule, inform them of what you expect from their child, how and when to contact you if necessary, and other information you deem pertinent. I would urge that you emphasize that any contact prior to or after any practice or game, is not permitted. Require them to schedule an individual, private meeting with you that is convenient for both parties. If a parent wants to attend practices, I leave that decision to you. Personally, I wanted my practices as private as possible. I made exceptions, but spectators were not allowed to talk, just listen, and watch.

CHAPTER 21

MOTIVATION AND QUOTES

For any coach to obtain any measure of success in the game of basketball, I strongly believe that they must, without exception, dwell on fundamental instruction. I have passed on in earlier chapters, many beliefs that greatly sided my teams to achieve the favorability they did. I also believe that there is a place for the intangible, that which is not perceptible to touch, in one's coaching style. No, this is not as important as instructions in the tools of the sport. However, sometimes it is necessary to sit your squad down and talk to them, motivate them, explain to them or give them a "wake up" call. It is a long season, including preseason and post season. In my junior college days, it lasted from the beginning of October to mid-March, almost six months.

This is a long stretch for a group to meet almost daily. There is an old saying, "Familiarity breeds contempt." It can occur with a basketball team. I said in Chapter 3, depending on the situation, it is often wise to give your squad down time. Meet in a classroom without practice gear and conduct a review of the season to date.

Such a session gives you the opportunity to be positive and make corrections. Do not make these meetings long as you will lose the players' interest and rob them of their day off. On the other hand, these occasions present you, as coach, opportunism to relate to these individuals some life goals, examples of other successes, why basketball and competition are a mirror of society and how usable habits are formed with the team format.

I am a strong advocate in adages. Below are some motivational famous quotes I have used to illustrate a point. Of course, there are numerous others. I list these for your use as you determine. Modestly, I include some of mine. I hope they are useful.

BASKETBALL & GENERAL SPORTS QUOTES

- THERE ARE NO SHORT CUTS TO ANY PLACE WORTHWHILE.
  Beverly Sills
- THERE IS NO GAIN WITHOUT PAIN.
  Ben Franklin
- THE MORE I PRACTICE, THE LUCKIER I GET.
  Gary Player
- I CAN ACCEPT FAILURE; EVERYONE FAILS AT SOMETHING, I CAN'T ACCEPT NOT TRYING.
  Michael Jordan
- BASKETBALL IS LIKE PHOTOGRAPHY, IF YOU DON'T FOCUS, ALL YOU HAVE IS THE NEGATIVE.
  Dan Frisby
- ONE DAY OF PRACTICE IS LIKE ONE DAY OF CLEAN LIVING, IT DOESN'T DO YOU ANY GOOD.   Abe Lemons
- SUCCESS IS THE SUM OF SMALL EFFORTS, REPEATED DAY IN AND DAY OUT.
  Robert Collier
- IF YOU WANT TEAM PLAY, YOU MUST STRESS DEFENSE. DEFENSE MAKES PLAYERS UNSELFISH.   John Brady
- I LIKE CRITICISM. IT MAKES YOU STRONG.
  LeBron James

- WHAT TO DO WITH A MISTAKE, RECOGNIZE IT, ADMIT IT, LEARN FROM IT, FORGET IT. <u>Dean Smith</u>

The following are quotes of mine that I have used quite often during the course of my coaching career. I hope one or two strike a chord with you.

- YOU EARN YOUR JOB BETWEEN THE BLACK LINES DURING DAILY PRACTICE SESSIONS.
- LOSERS ALIBI, WINNERS WORK!
- YOU MUST PRACTICE LIKE YOU HAVE TO PLAY.
- IT IS A PRIVILEGE TO PRACTICE.
- WINNERS DO WHAT LOSERS NEGLECT!
- WE WANT GOOD RESULTS, NOT EXCUSES.
- GOOD DEFENSE IS PREVENTION OF MISTAKES, NOT REACTING TO THEM.
- THERE IS ONLY ONE BALL FOR FIVE PLAYERS, SHARE IT.
- I DO NOT RUN A DEMOCRACY ON WHO PLAYS. I MAKE THAT DECISION AS A "DICTATOR" WITHOUT A VOTE!
- DO NOT MERELY BOUNCE THE BALL. ELIMINATE THE ONE BOUNCE HABIT.
- WHEN AT PRACTICE YOU ARE ATTENDING BASKETBALL CLASS, TREAT EACH ONE AS SUCH.
- WITH DISCIPLINE I ATTEMPT TO BE FIRM, BUT FAIR.

- SWEAT & SACRIFICE SPELL SUCCESS (The 4 S's)
- NEVER REST ON DEFENSE, NEVER MEANS NEVER!!
- IF YOU WANT PLAYING TIME, TAKE SOMEONE'S JOB
- FORGET THE SUMMERTIME TROT WHEN RETREATING ON DEFENSE, SPRINT BACK EVERY TIME!
- YOU DO NOT HAVE TO LIKE ME, JUST RESPECT ME AND WHAT I AM ATTEMPTING TO TEACH.
- WHENEVER I AM CORRECTING OR COACHING A PLAYER, I AM INSTRUCTING ALL, LISTEN!
- WHEN I BLOW MY WHISTLE, STOP AND LISTEN.

CHAPTER 22 - Diagrams

SHELL DRILL

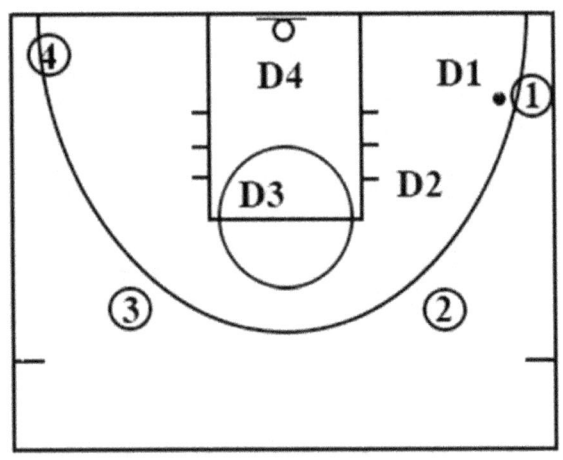

Diagram 1

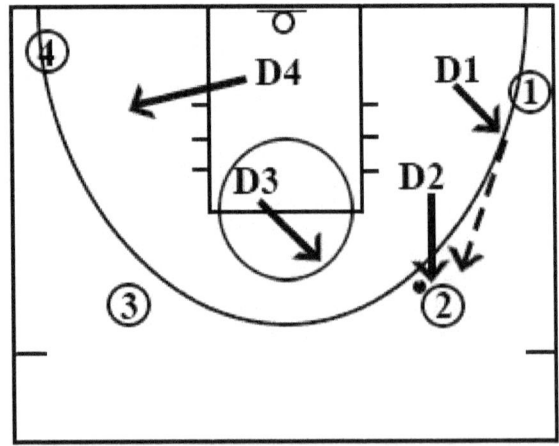

Diagram 2

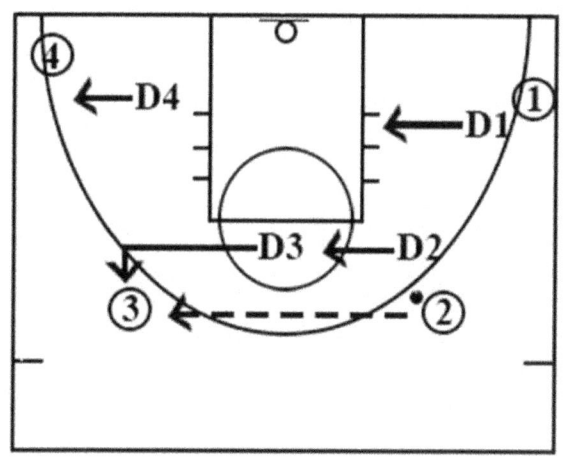

Diagram 3

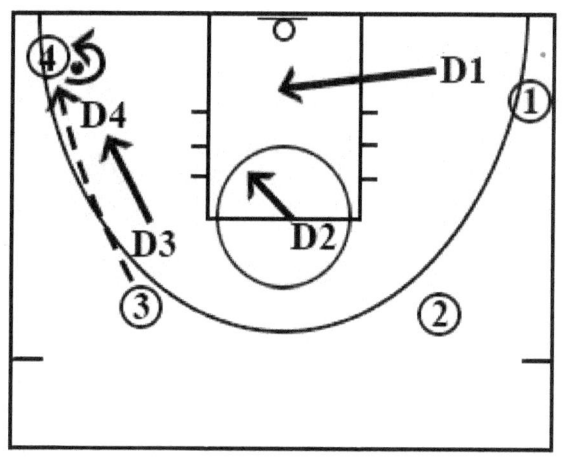

Diagram 4

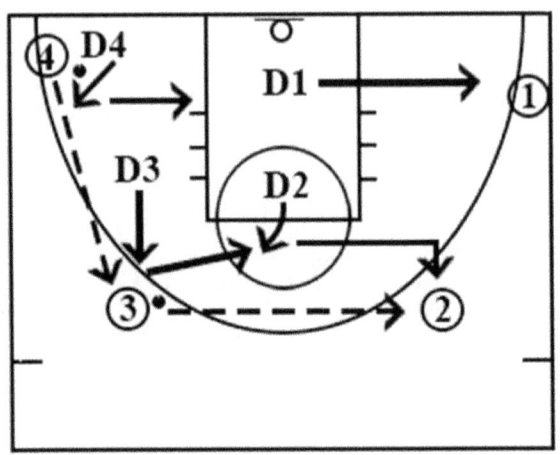

Diagram 5

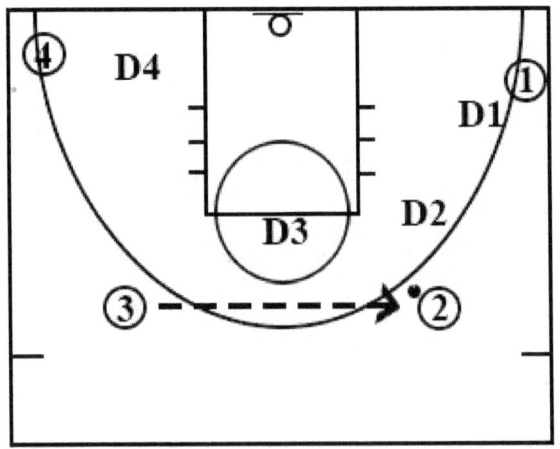

Diagram 6

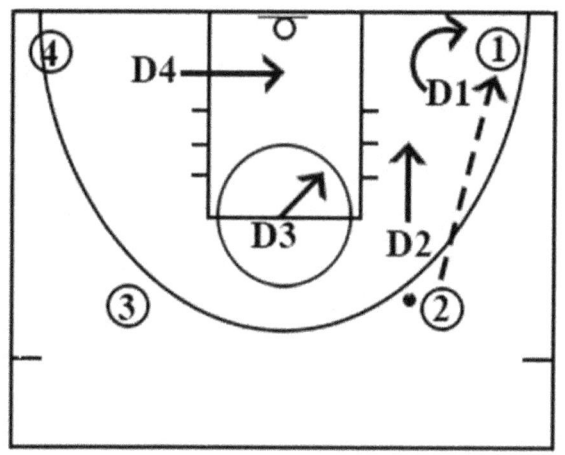

Diagram 7

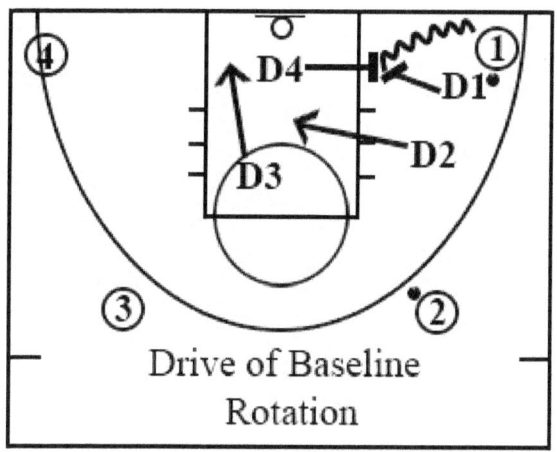

Drive of Baseline Rotation

Diagram 8

2-1-2 ZONE SLIDES

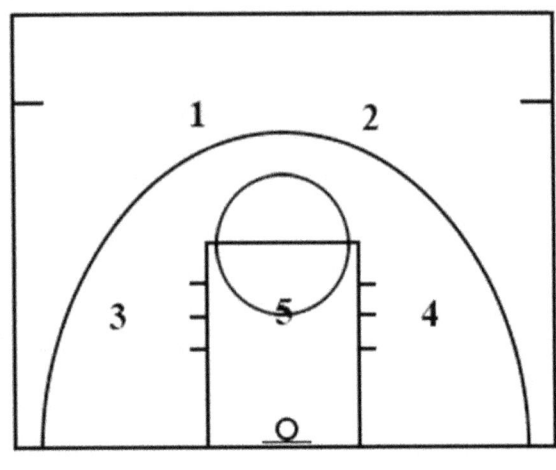

Diagram 1

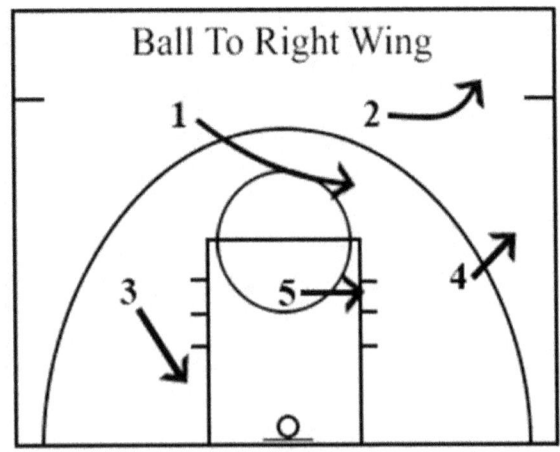

Diagram 2

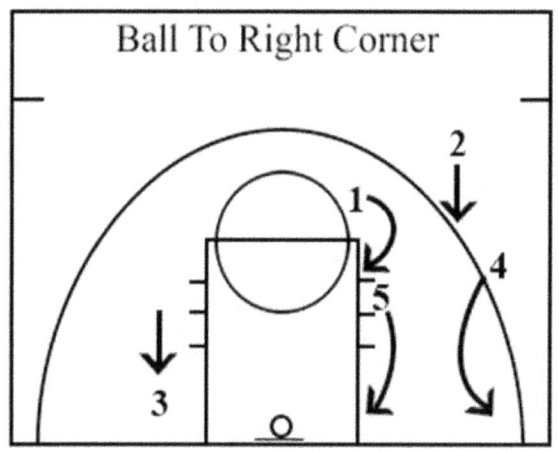

Diagram 3

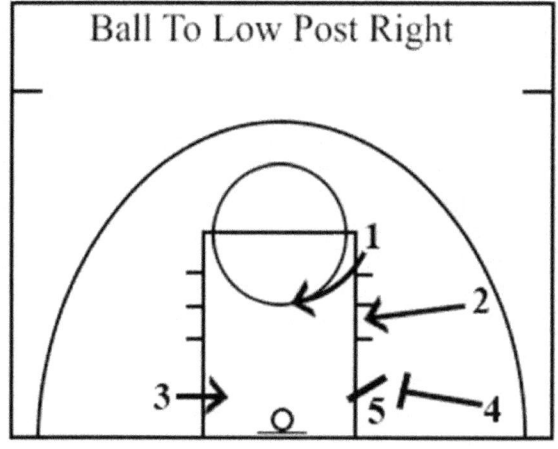

Diagram 4

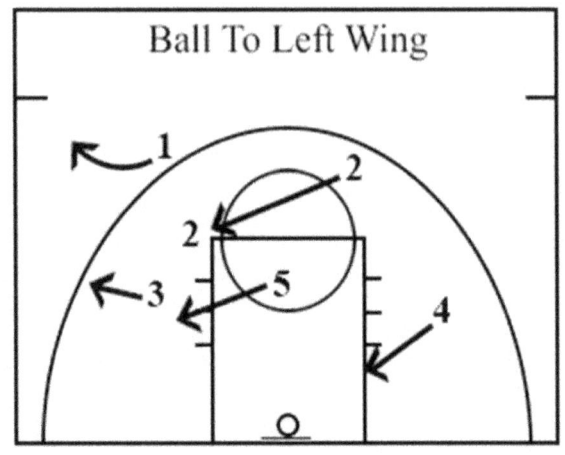

Diagram 5

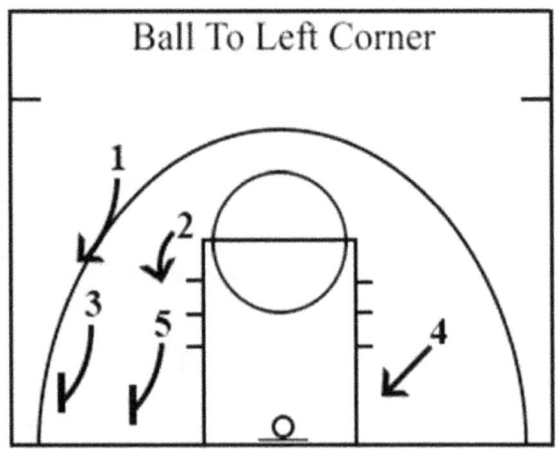

Diagram 6

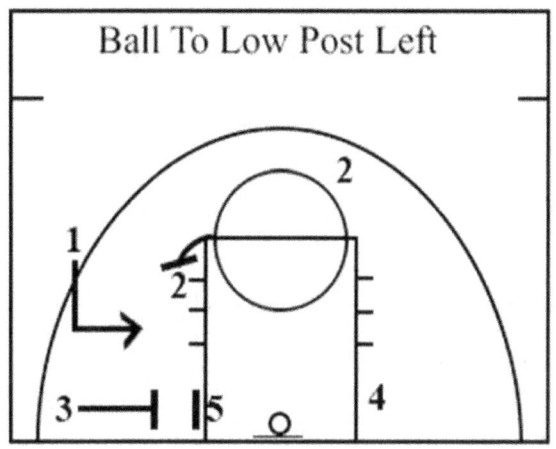

Diagram 7

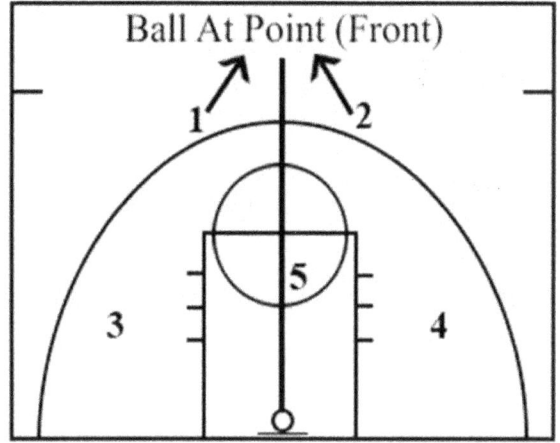

Diagram 8

1-3-1 ZONE SLIDES

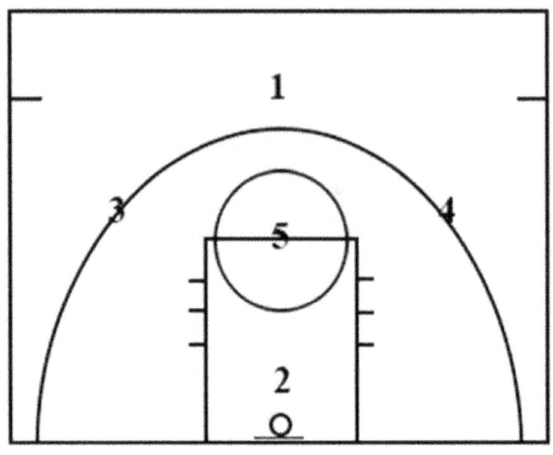

Diagram 1

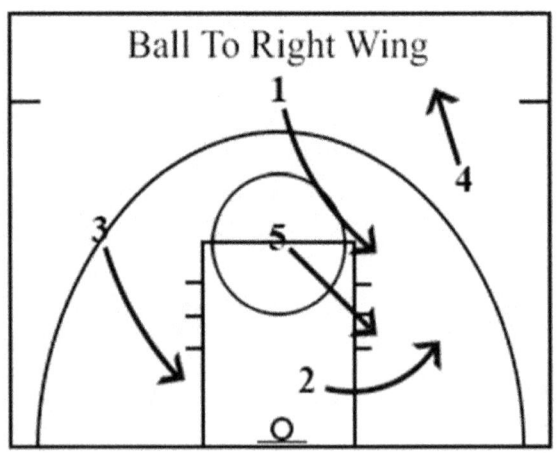

Diagram 2

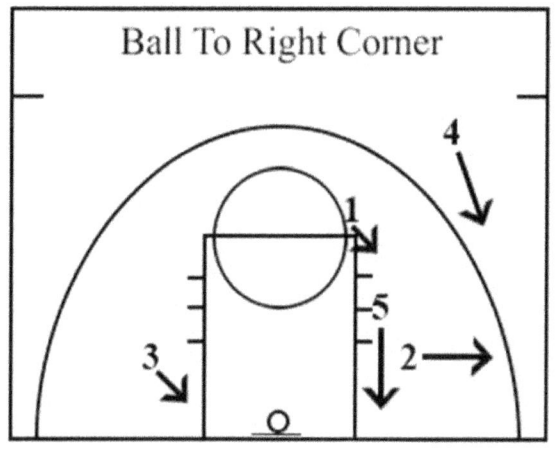

Diagram 3

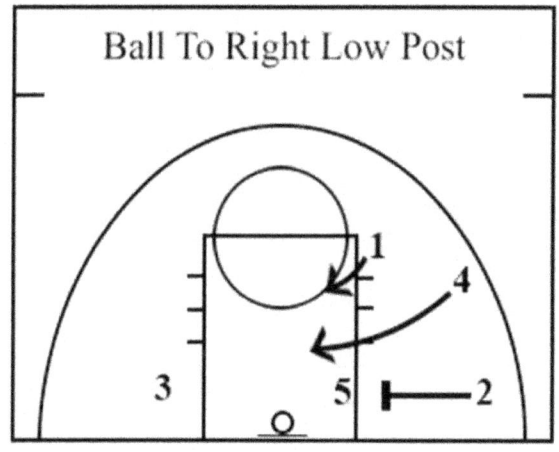

Diagram 4

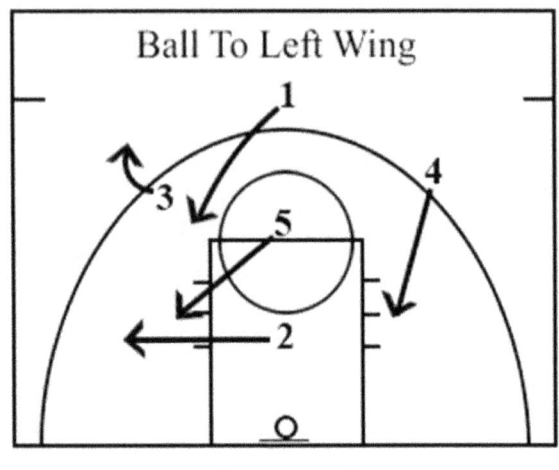

Diagram 5

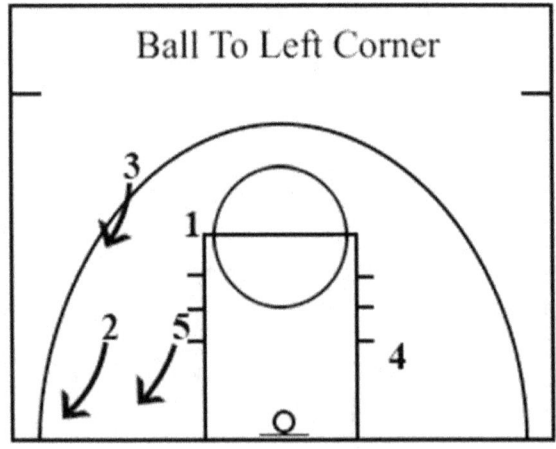

Diagram 6

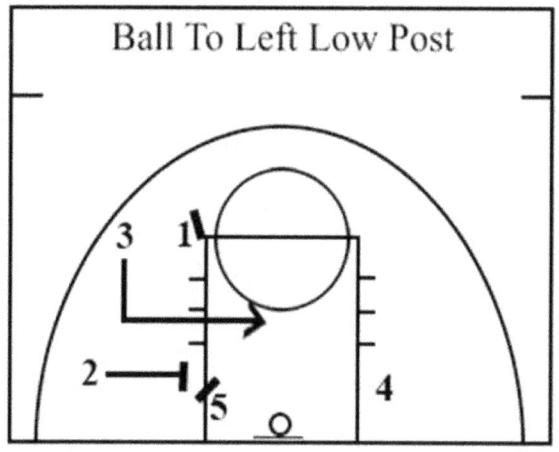

Diagram 7

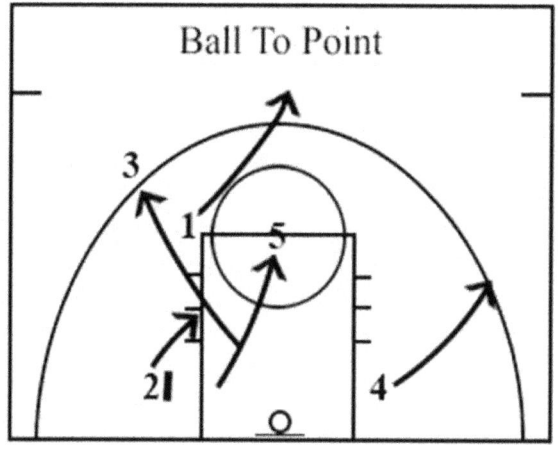

Diagram 8

T-DEFENSE FROM 2-3 ZONE

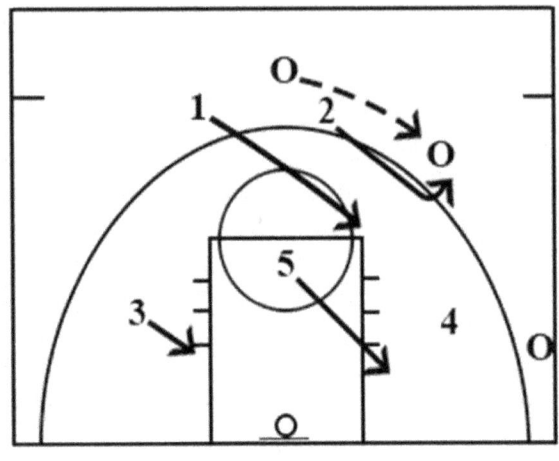

Diagram 1

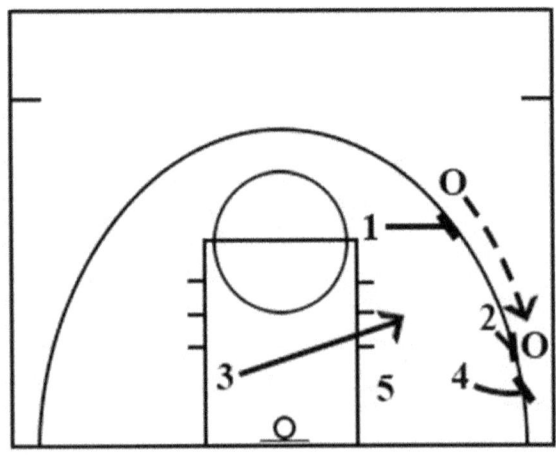

Diagram 2

T-DEFENSE FROM 1-3-1 ZONE

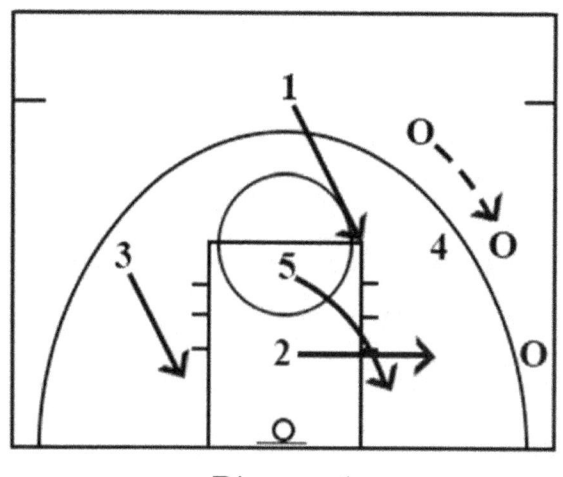

Diagram 1

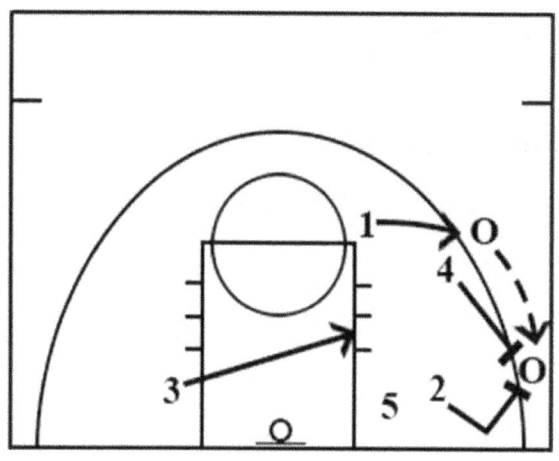

Diagram 2

BLUE OFFENSE

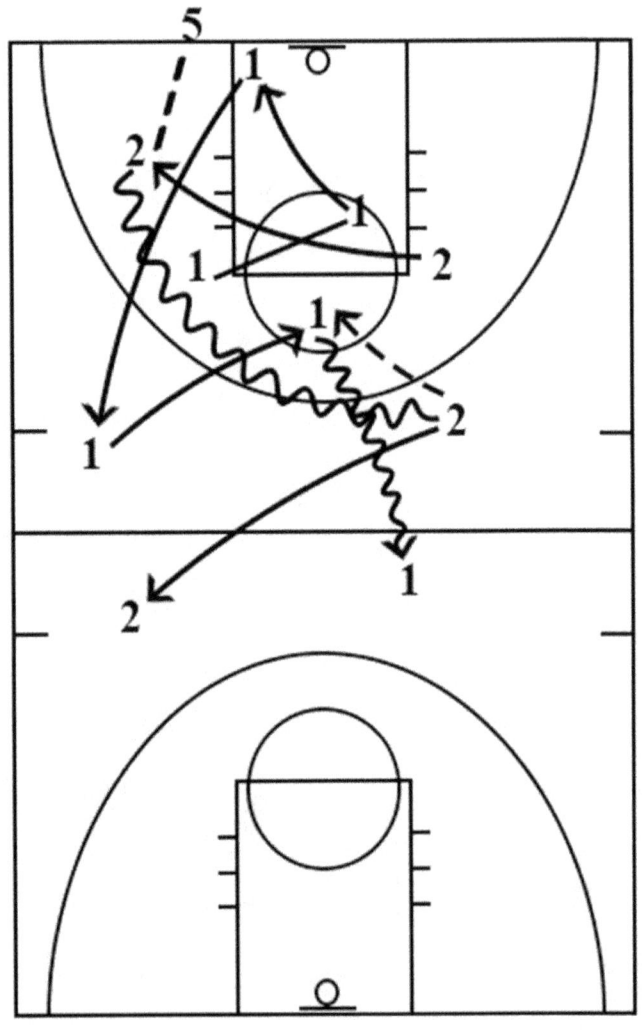

Diagram 1

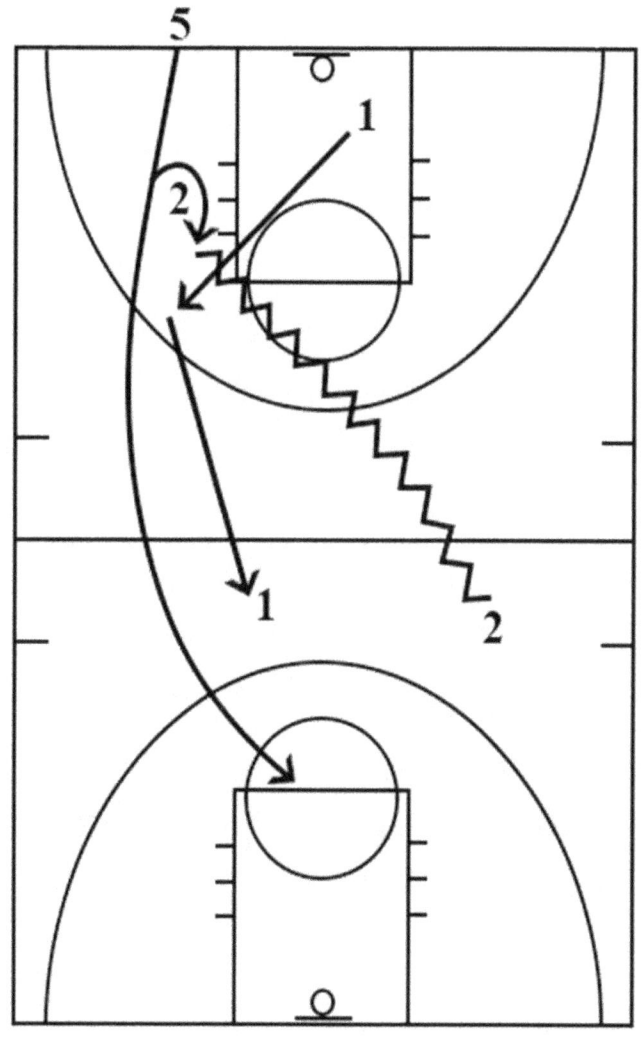

Diagram 2

CUT & HOOK BACK

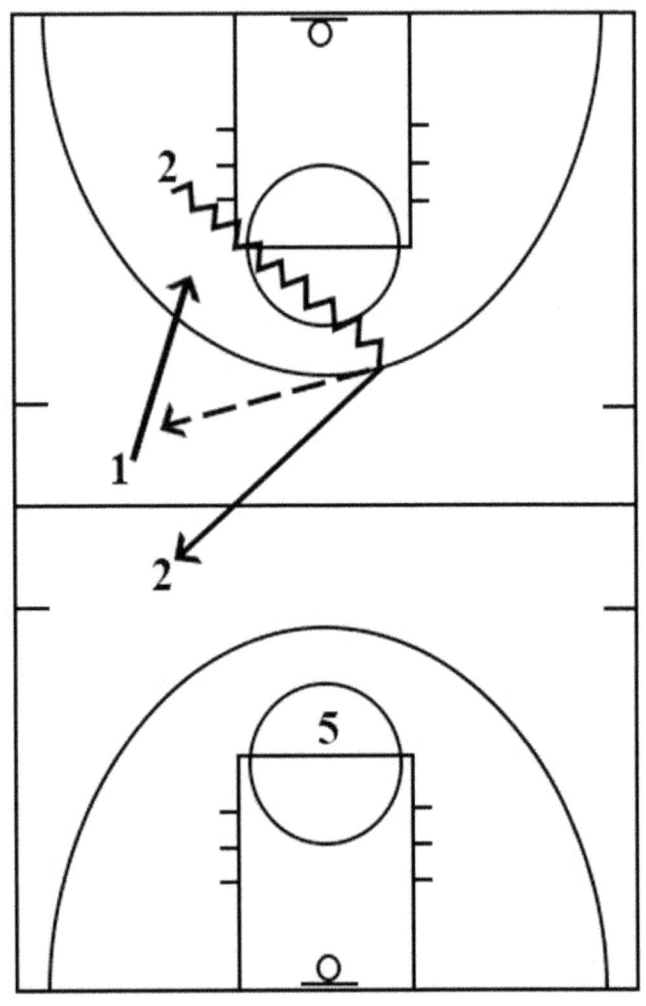

Diagram 1

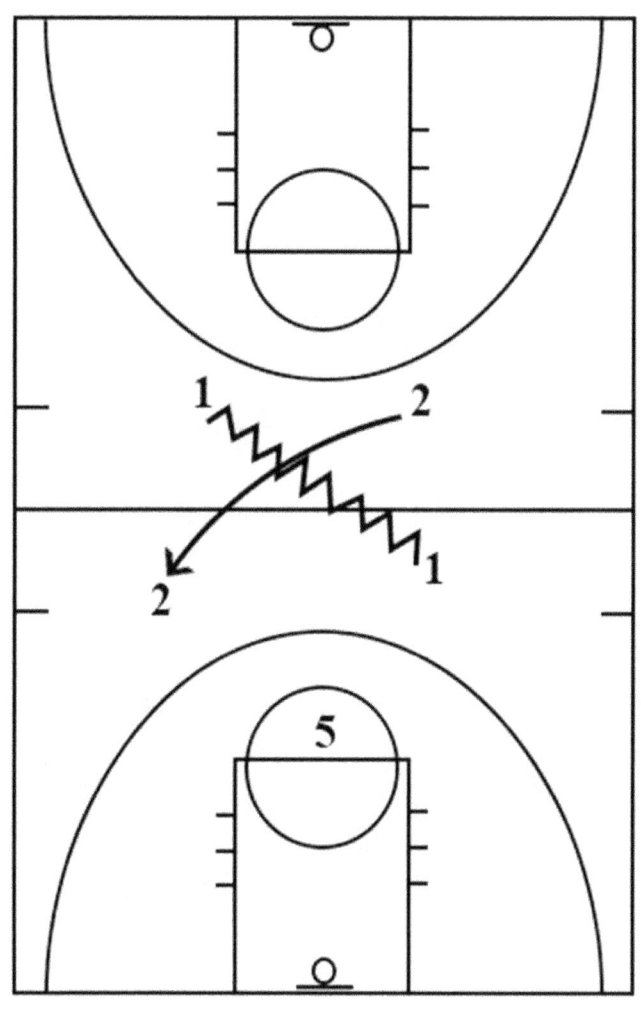

Diagram 2

SET UP & MOVES TO BEAT ZONE PRESS

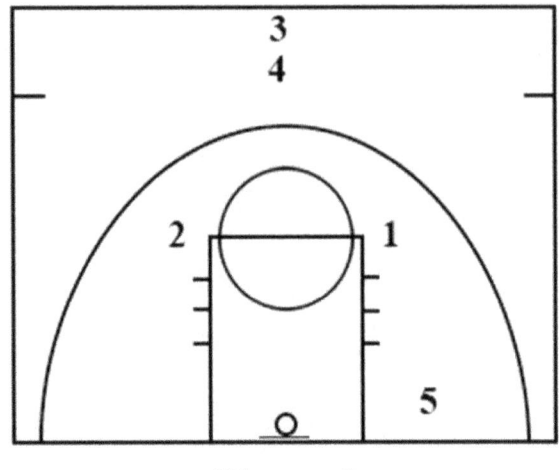

Diagram 1

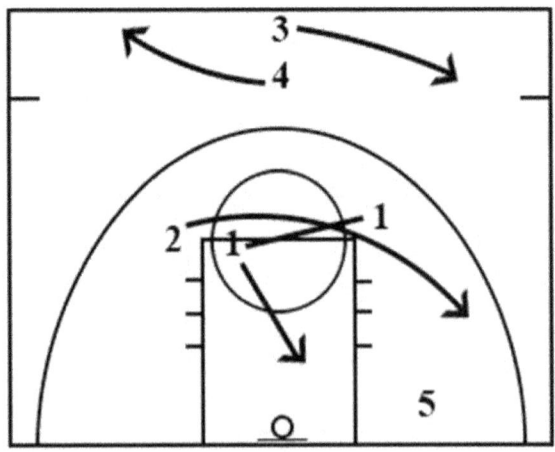

Diagram 2

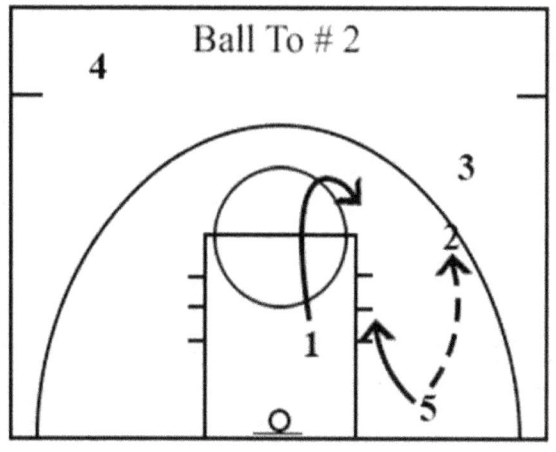

Diagram 3

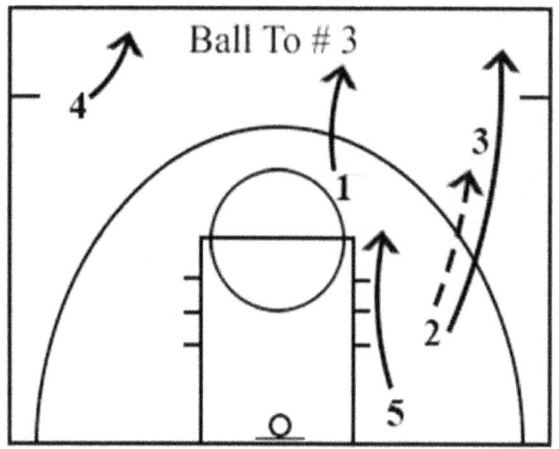

Diagram 4

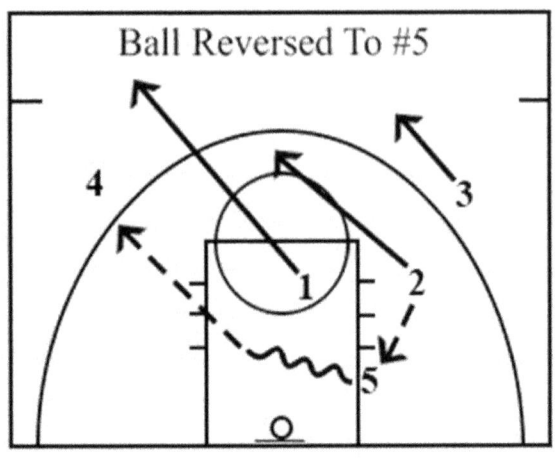

Diagram 5

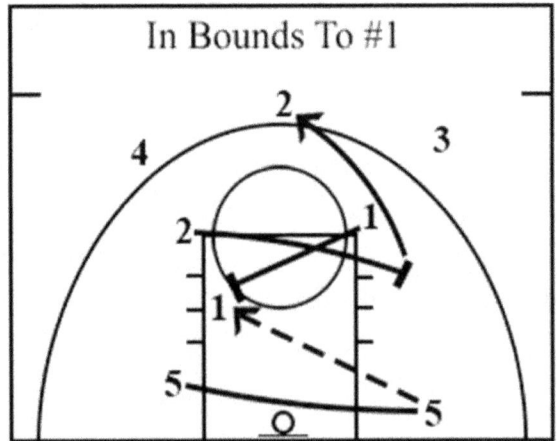

Diagram 6

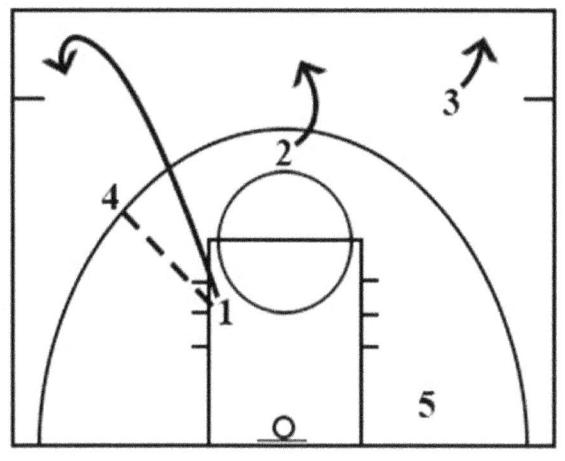

Diagram 6

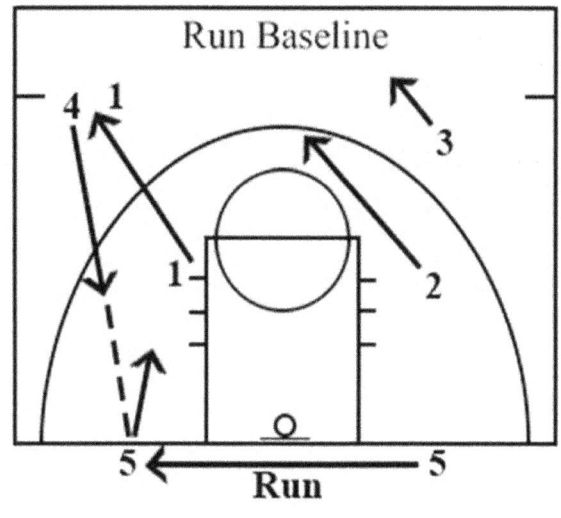

Diagram 8

EPILOGUE

The dictionary defines epilogue as, "A concluding section that rounds out the design of a literary work." I do not believe this "work" is bookish or literary. Nor do I know how many will have the chance to read my words. I did not put this information on paper for profit or notoriety. The game of basketball has given me many fond memories as a player, referee, coach, and lifetime fan. As I grow older, and I am now 92. I have increasingly gained the desire to give back. I feel I have been blessed with sound physical and mental health. I performed several volunteer services since starting this book. I have spent one day a week at a senior assisted living center for several years. I am an elected elder at my church. I have also assisted the head varsity basketball coach at the local high school. All these activities gave me pleasure and a sense of worth in the twilight of my life.

Several years ago, I said to myself, "Why not write a book?" This endeavor has been a labor of love, and as much, to be included in that list of giving back. Nothing more! It has taken longer than I thought it would. Though I confess, "It was not my priority at times and there were some lengthy periods of neglect." However, the urge never left me.

One of the true rewards in life is the reality that along the way you made a difference. As one travels that path, a person is not cognizant of that possibility.

You just do your job day by day. As I look back, I believe that was me. I now realize that there is evidence that I did make a difference in the lives of some people. Who? I have former players scattered throughout this country, and even one in Israel and another in Australia. What do I hear from them via emails, phone calls, and sometimes, in person? All tell me emphatically, sincerely and lovingly, "Coach, you made such a difference in my life. Thank you!" I jokingly reply these days, "I hear this so often, I am prone to believing it." Though seriously, they are words that warm my heart. Words that are the true rewards of a life well spent. Here is one example I received recently at Christmas.

"Basketball like other sports is a game heaped in stats. Wins, losses, shot %, rebounds, turnovers, but when those whistles stop blowing and all that is left is time to reflect on MOMENTS, that's when Coach Phipps comes to center stage. You rank way up there on the list of gifts bestowed upon me by our Lord. And all those life principles that you engrained in me and my teammates have endured, and I have shared them with every young person who has crossed my path. This is the season of Giving and Gratitude. So, thanks for your time, love, strength, and knowledge. You will never be forgotten."

Just imagine the joy and smile on my face as I read that email. I have been the recipient of many similar messages since retirement. I would be remiss if I omitted from the final thoughts any mention of my former players. I do so now, not individually, but as a group. I remember saying to many of you, "I realize I am not easy to play for because of my demands." Hopefully, I say now in all heartful sincerity, "THANK YOU, ONE AND ALL!" for your loyalty, hard work, enthusiasm, and dedication to purpose. Each and every one of you made our team the one to be reckoned with every season. You took pride in your victories and were gracious in your losses. It was indeed an honor and privilege to be your coach. Blessings to all.

I will end with a poem that I have taken liberties with. I first read the original when attending a Fellowship of Christian Athletes summer conference in 1964 at Henderson Harbor, New York. It was printed in a brochure. It was reprinted with the kind permission of Mrs. E.G. Wright. I am not sure if she is the author or maybe her husband. The original's theme concerned football. I have substituted basketball and basketball terminology. I believe it sums up adequately this period of time we call life.

THE BIG GAME

Life is like a game of basketball
And you play it every day.
It isn't just the breaks you get
But how well do you play?

Stop and look the whole team over
You have some pretty rugged men
If you work them all together
There is not a goal you cannot defend.

Your center's name is Courage,
You will need him in this game.
With Truth and Faith your forwards
There will be many points to gain.

Your playmaker is very fast
Though small and hard to see
So, watch when he gets the ball,
He is Opportunity.

At one guard there is Religion
He has stood the test of time.
On the bench there is Brotherhood
He's in there always trying.

Another sub is Ambition
Don't ever let him shirk.
That hustler you call sixth man
You will find his name is Work.

Another teammate's name is Humor
He is important to this team.
While Honor playing at every position
Your game is always clean.

If Love is in the coach's spot
And does his very best.
Then you will have a winning team
And really know success.

The other team is tough, my friend,
Greed, Envy, Hatred, and Defeat
Are four strong for you to conquer
To make your game complete.

Discouragement and Falsehood are others
With whom you will have to contend
You will have to play very hard,
When you meet up with these men.

Selfishness and Jealousy, if you look,
You will find them playing guard,
While Carelessness and one called Waste
Are two corner men you cannot disregard.

There is one more you'll have to watch
All through the game, my dear.
He is playing center for this team
I am told his name is Fear.

This game will not be easy:
There will be struggle and be strife.
To make the winning basket
For its played in the gymnasium of Life.

So stand behind your team, Son,
There will be many who will applaud.
Just remember… you are the Captain:
And the Referee… is GOD!

ABOUT THE AUTHOR

Jerry Phipps is a well-respected head basketball coach with nearly four decades of experience coaching at the high school and junior college level. Inducted into four Halls of Fame over his career and chosen as the Region 20 of the National Junior College Association "Coach of the Year" for five seasons, Phipps has built an impressive reputation both on and off the court. During his career, he garnered over 700 wins and earned the highest winning percentage among all NJCAA basketball coaches with a record close to 80 percent at retirement.

Phipps experience with the game started as a player during high school and college. As head coach for the Baltimore City College Black Knights, he achieved an overall record of 133 wins and 28 losses. He led the Black Knights to victory for the first time since 1939, securing four Maryland Scholastic championship titles during his eight-year tenure. They also added two undefeated seasons of 20-0 and a 40-game- winning streak to their record. In his last seven seasons as head coach, the Black Nights never finished lower than tied for 1st place in their own divisional league play.

Phipps went on to serve as head basketball coach for the Baltimore Community College Red Devils. There he achieved an overall record of 360 wins and 87 losses. Under his 14-year leadership, the Red Devils took home 12 Maryland JUCO championship titles. Additionally, they won five Region 20 titles of the NJCAA.

After retirement, Phipps went on to coach for Essex Community College; Woodlawn, John Carol, and Hickey high schools. Beloved by his former students, he prides himself on not only teaching the game but teaching life lessons as well. In 2015, he relocated to Vero Beach, Florida. Where at age 85, he continued to coach to help young players. Through this work, Phipps hopes to contribute to the game that he has grown to love and respect over a lifetime.

www.ingramcontent.com/pod-product-compliance
Lightning Source LLC
LaVergne TN
LVHW051828080426
835512LV00018B/2776